Connections Book Two

# MAGGIE

GW00673722

Katharine E. Smith

## HEDDON PUBLISHING

First edition published in 2022 by Heddon Publishing.

ISBN 978-1-913166-57-1
Ebook 978-1-913166-56-4

Cover design by Catherine Clarke Design
www.catherineclarkedesign.co.uk

www.heddonpublishing.com
www.facebook.com/heddonpublishing
@PublishHeddon

 Katharine E. Smith is the author of thirteen novels, including the bestselling Coming Back to Cornwall series. *Maggie* is the second book of the Connections series – also set in Cornwall but quite different.

A Philosophy graduate, Katharine initially worked in the IT and charity sectors. She turned to freelance editing in 2009, which led to her setting up Heddon Publishing, working with independent authors across the globe.

Katharine lives in Shropshire, UK, with her husband, their two children, and their border collie.

You can find details of her books on her website:
www.katharineesmith.com

Information about her work with other authors can be found here:
www.heddonpublishing.com
and
www.heddonbooks.com

For Margaret Schroder
with a whole lot of love xx

# MAGGIE

# Maggie

I am starting to feel really bad that I haven't been entirely honest with Elise. It's just that, as time goes on, it's becoming increasingly difficult to tell the truth. And I know she's got this particular image of me, which I haven't done much to correct. To her, I'm just a hard-working single mum, with an unsupportive family, and Stevie is the product of a failed relationship with an unreliable, useless man.

Now, some of these things are true. I am a hard-working single mum, and Stevie's dad is completely unreliable, and useless, at least as far as I'm concerned. But then that is only a part of the truth. As with many people's stories, it's not altogether straightforward. And I worry what Elise would say if she knew the whole of it.

I like the 'me' that she sees. Especially compared to how my (former) best friend, and my own mum and sister, might feel about me. Not Mum, maybe, but certainly Julia and Stacey.

And I never meant to lie to Elise, but when we talked that time, at Lanhydrock, and I started to get an idea of what her marriage had been like, I just couldn't bear to tell her the whole truth. She has been through so much, and been so strong. And I've just been a fool. But for some reason, I let her think otherwise. I suppose I liked her sympathy.

There have been times when I've hated myself, but I know that's of no use, and I seem to have inherited Dad's ability to bounce back. A survivor's instinct. Which is important for me, and for Stevie. I may have let down most of the people I love, but I've never let her down, and I don't intend to start now.

This is why I'm taking it slowly with Tony. I do really like him, but we've been there before, haven't we? Honestly, I can physically cringe when I think of what I've been like in the past. Always so keen for boys to like me at school, when I knew deep down that they really only wanted to know me to get closer to Stacey, or Julia. It only made me try harder. Like I say – cringe.

So I'll take it slow. Until I get to know him. His past. Does he have secrets of his own? He's been married, he says, no kids. Why is this? Did they not want them? Did he want them, and not her? Or the other way round? Was he a philanderer? A work-addict? A good, old-fashioned bastard?

I feel bad thinking those things about him, but really, I don't know him, do I? I suppose, if this lasts, and if he really is all that he seems to be, I will have to face telling him the truth, too. Maybe he'll pass all of my requirements – I hesitate to say 'tests' – with flying colours, and then I'll blow it all with the truth about me, and alienate him like I've alienated all the other people I care about. Except for Stevie. And now Elise. And what will happen when Elise finds out, as I suppose she must?

I just can't let Stevie know the truth. I can't bear her to see me for the weak woman I am. But I'm kidding myself if I think we can go through life without her finding out. And I can't keep her away from Mum, or Julia, forever. I just hope they do still care enough about me, or Stevie at the very least, to keep their mouths shut.

I'm getting quite stressed out, thinking about it all. Putting all the personal stuff aside, very soon I am going to have to tell Elise about my job, and who I'm working for, because it's going to be obvious. But having heard all the incredibly strong – almost unanimously negative – opinions about the Saltings, around town and while I was volunteering at Caring the Community, when the truth comes out about my new role, I fear I'm not going to be very popular.

Tied up with this new development, changing the face of the town forever. I've been offered a great job, and I genuinely think I can help make everything work better for people in the town. I just know it won't be seen like that, though. I am scared I'll be seen as a traitor, just when I'm starting to feel at home here.

# 1991

"Make your own friends, girls," the twins' mum had tried to warn Maggie and Julia. "Don't try to share – not your best friend, anyway. Three is difficult. Take it from me."

But they had not wanted to listen to Lucy. They both wanted Stacey Pattern for their best friend, and neither was willing to give her up. Stacey was an only child, who seemed to exude confidence, as though she could find her place anywhere, and that place would always be at the top. An adult might easily see that she needed Maggie and Julia as much as they needed her – very possibly more. After all, they had each other, and they had supportive, interested parents, whereas Stacey had no siblings, and parents who were good at providing money, and clothes, and a host of pets, but were not quite so interested in spending actual time with her. Still, to her peers, Stacey had it all, and she did her best to keep that appearance up. She made a beeline for the twins, with their ready-made link of their dads being workmates, and the girls felt flattered, that this outgoing, confident girl had chosen them. So, the eleven-year-old twins had agreed to share their friend as they shared most other things – starting with their parents and also including their clothes, their sense of humour, and even their room (despite the fact that their new house had a third bedroom, which one of them could have had, but which instead sat full of boxes that nobody could quite bring themselves to unpack just yet).

Stacey and the twins had just somehow gravitated

towards each other; all being completely new, not just to secondary school but to the whole area. Just on the Cornwall side of the Devon-Cornwall border, the town was big enough for a secondary school, the intake being from the two moderately-sized primaries, and a range of small schools in the outlying villages.

The twins and their parents had moved down from Bristol, while Stacey's family had come all the way from Leeds. The twins' dad, Jeff, and Stacey's dad, Rob, were both newly employed at a fast-growing engineering and manufacturing firm. Both families had seized the chance to fulfil long-held dreams of living by the sea, and the girls' friendship sparked a relationship between their parents. There were beach days and barbecues well into the evenings. Dinners at each other's houses, sleepovers, and birthday parties. It wasn't just the girls who were feeling slightly out of place in this small rural town. The two families found a strength in each other. Even though Rob was Jeff's boss, it didn't matter. Not at first, anyway.

Jeff and Lucy had always wanted the girls to have their own personalities and different interests.

"Just because you're twins, and look the same, it doesn't mean you *are* the same, or have to be the same," Lucy told them. ("Better for them to be different – then hopefully there won't be as much comparison between them as they get older," she said to Jeff, "from other people, or between themselves.")

And to some extent this was the case. Julia liked ballet and gym, while Maggie enjoyed running and swimming and, as she grew older, skateboarding.

Stacey met them somewhere down the middle, going to gym with Julia, and pipping Maggie to the post in the first swimming gala they attended together. Maggie didn't mind too much. Especially when Stacey hugged her afterwards. "You were so much better than all the others," Stacey said, and Maggie had glowed at the apparent compliment.

Julia, however, topped Stacey at gymnastics and ballet, but, as her body changed, she gave up the ballet to concentrate on other forms of dance. In time, gymnastics fell by the wayside, too. Stacey cut her losses, realising she could not beat Julia, and so she decided to concentrate on swimming, where she knew she would win; her small, lithe body cutting through the water with ease. Maggie just carried on, accepting that she was always going to be second place. If she was very honest, a small part of her wished that things were different, but, as Jeff often said, it was better to be happy with who she was, and what she could do, than comparing herself to other people and what they were capable of.

The problem was, that despite their parents' best efforts, it was almost inevitable, growing up, that the girls would compare themselves: to other people, and to each other. In advising them not to do so, their parents missed the chance to discuss these things, and talk their daughters through them. Perhaps, deep down, they found themselves comparing their own lives, and their own jobs, and their house, to Rob and Sarah's. And not always finding favourable results. But they would never admit it – not to each other, and not even to themselves.

# Maggie

I will start by telling Elise about the job. It's not like I can hide it for much longer, anyway. I start in two weeks' time. I'm sad it's going to cut through Stevie's school holiday – I have always loved the summer breaks – and this time it's the last one before she starts at secondary school. It's hard to believe, somehow. But needs must, and when this job opportunity presented itself, I realised that there may not be another like it. It's a fantastic job, too. Working with Canyon Holdings, who have bank-rolled the Saltings development, to create closer ties to the community. A cynic might say it's all in their interest; the fewer objections they have, the more they can get away with. But if you look at things a different way, this is them being socially responsible, and trying to ensure that they impact the local community positively. This is how I'm choosing to look at it, and if I'm on the inside, I can help to make sure that this is how it works out.

Besides, I need to earn some money, and I need to do something with my time, now that Stevie's growing up. And I want to work. I miss it. I enjoy the sense of purpose, and the sense of orderliness that can be achieved in work. Motherhood is the best thing that has ever happened to me, but I've had to learn that there is so much outside my control, or which changes rapidly and unexpectedly. I've never really been very good at just 'rolling with it', but I have had to teach myself to, or at least to give the appearance of it. Inside, I might be on edge and stressed, with a constant 'to do' list like a roll of till receipt, but on the outside I'll try my best to be calm and cool and collected. That is what my daughter needs to see. I don't suppose I'll ever have the career I once imagined, but I'm not sure that's what I want now anyway.

When I was offered this new job, I allowed myself some moments of elation, and then I let the worries in. They have since been gnawing away at me, and I've found myself imagining what people will say when they hear I'm working for the enemy. During my time at Caring the Community (I really wish they'd change that name), and from scrolling through the local Facebook group page, I've heard and seen so many complaints and criticisms about the Saltings, and the incomers from London and beyond, trampling all over the town, changing the face of it, pricing youngsters out of the housing market (that ship has long since sailed, though). When I'm on my own, which is a lot of the time, I have found myself imagining the kind of comments which might be levelled at me. And then the replies I might come up with, which would floor my opponent, and possibly earn a round of applause (or hundreds of Likes).

In reality, I absolutely hate face-to-face confrontations, and I might have typed out a few replies to Facebook comments in the past, but I've never actually posted them.

"My new job's for the Saltings," I blurt out, unrehearsed, when Elise puts a cup of tea on the table in front of me.

"Is it, now?" she asks, sitting across from me and seeming utterly unsurprised.

"Yes, do you hate me?" I look at her; meet her eyes; see only her usual mild, friendly smile.

"Of course I don't. And did you think I hadn't already worked that out, my love? There's not many jobs going round here, for the likes of you. Unless it's with the council, or something. I thought, when you mentioned it, that it was strange you hadn't said who you were working for. But I thought I'd wait for you to tell me."

"Oh my god, Elise. I can't believe you! I thought you'd be annoyed with me. I know why people hate the development. I get it. But my new job – and it's not really just admin, there's loads more to it – is all about trying to make the Saltings a good thing for the community." I can feel the earnestness in my voice, and want to shake myself. I feel like a child looking for approval.

"Maggie!" she laughs, and leans forward, putting her hand on mine. "You do not have to justify anything to me. You've got a young daughter to look after, and a good brain to use. I don't hate the Saltings. Times change, places change, people have to get on with it. So don't you worry about me, and what I might think, for one moment more. Some of the other oldies might take a little more persuading, but you're doing them a favour, giving them something new to complain about!"

I can't help laughing now as well. I should have known, really, that she wouldn't think any the worse of me. I've done my usual thing of letting something become more of a problem in my head than it actually is in reality.

"Besides," she says, "The company my daughter Louisa works for has something to do with the Saltings, or Canyon Holdings. I don't know exactly what. She did tell me, but I'm afraid I let it all go over my head. Still, it would be a bit hypocritical of me to judge you for working for them."

"I didn't know that, about Louisa."

"Oh yes, it was one of the reasons she came down here for a whole week – well that and the American chap she was seeing. He's all tied up with it, too. Maybe you'll meet him! Anyway, tell me what you're actually going to be doing."

I sit back in my chair, telling myself to relax, and I explain the ins and outs of the job, not in too much detail, but I don't dumb it down, either. "It's all about them taking on social responsibility. Recognising the impact they're having on the local community and trying to make sure it works for everyone. There are going to be some grants for local groups – maybe Caring the Community will get one – and a community room, plus a work space for small businesses to use, for meetings and so on. We—" I might as well start including myself in this — "want to link up with the local job centre, and residential homes; maybe have dementia-friendly cinema screenings. There's more scope for all this in the quieter months, but Canyon are committed to making provisions for local people all year round."

I feel like I'm in an advert. But I can also feel some passion in me, and enthusiasm, for what I'm about to become involved with. There is so much going on around here, once you start to look. The local quarterly magazine has a long list of groups to join, from book clubs to a men's shed, but there could be so much more, with the right funding and facilities. I really feel like my job could be part of something great.

"Now, tell me about Stevie. And how's this going to work with the school holidays? Will you need a babysitter?" Elise changes the subject and I realise that one of the things I've been so anxious about has turned out to be so much less important than I had feared. I am very good at letting my fears grow and spin out of control. Especially when I think it might make people like me less. How much valuable time I waste worrying, normally about things that never come to fruition. To Elise, I realise, having our company is more important than any job I might have. I think I can feel some hope in her voice when she asks about babysitting.

"Ah, yes, well, it is bad timing, in that respect. I need to get thinking about how that will all work out." I've actually been talking to Mum about her coming down for part of the summer. She's got a friend with a place in a nearby town, and might be able to stay there. She is very keen to come and see Stevie and me, and I know she'd love to look after Stevie while I'm working. I don't want to tell Elise that just yet, though. Besides, she thinks my mum is not a great person – which is entirely untrue, and entirely my fault, because it's what I've led her to believe.

"Well, I'm always around if you need me," Elise says. "But I don't expect Stevie will want to spend all her summer with an old woman like me! You know, I'm sure there are holiday clubs; I've seen groups out and about in the town and on the beaches. There's a churchy one too, but I don't think that's your cup of tea."

"I will have a look into it all," I say, and feel myself tensing up again. "So much to do!"

"You'll do it," says Elise. "I know you will. And if you need a helping hand, I'm here."

"Thank you, Elise. You have no idea how much that means to me."

"Well, you have no idea how much you and Stevie mean to me."

As I walk home, I think of those words. I kick myself. I may have felt momentary relief at telling her about the job, but there are still more truths I've concealed from her. I wonder, not for the first time, why I told her what I did about my family, and the reasons I moved down here. I suppose I didn't want her to think badly of me, as I'm sure she would if she knew the truth. I was running away, from my own past mistakes – or mistake. Elise sees me as an uncomplicated, good person. And a fighter. A survivor. I like that.

But she has become more of a part of our lives than I'd anticipated, and once Mum is here, there is a very good chance that the two of them will meet. It won't take long for Elise to realise that I lied about the reasons I moved down here – and about my family life. That I've actually got the best family. That Dad died years ago. And that my mum absolutely adores Stevie, and misses her, and would love it if we moved back. But I've been keeping back the truth from Mum as well, and from Julia.

I've been so ashamed of myself, and the anxiety has been eating me up, but it would have been worse had I not moved away. Besides, I like it here. More than I knew that I would. I'm happier now, than I have been in some time. And I am starting to realise that, although I did something stupid, it was ill-judged, and in a time when I was vulnerable. Maybe it isn't me who should be ashamed.

But if I want to get on with my life, it's about time I owned up to it all, to all of them, or I'll forever be wrapping myself up in more lies, and that can't be good for any of us. I just need to find the right time.

# 1991

It was the day before the school Christmas disco. All three girls were excited about it, even though it was only being held in the school sports hall. And teachers would be chaperoning, of course. Not that the twins had any need for chaperoning, but there were definitely kids in their year who, if their reputations were to be believed, might need an extra eye on them. Would Stacey prove to be one of them? Maggie thought it wasn't out of the question.

Mr O'Connor, the boys' PE teacher, was 'on the decks', as he put it, to much eye-rolling from the first years. They were having an hour's disco to themselves, then would be allowed to leave school early, while the second- and third-years had their turn in the hall, and finally the fourth- and fifth-years. With each tranche of pupils, the number of teachers on hand increased, and there had been stern warnings to the upper years that there was a zero-tolerance attitude towards alcohol.

"Alcohol? At school?" Lucy had queried, at the dinner table. "They wouldn't, would they?"

Jeff had chuckled. "Oh love, your convent education becomes apparent again!"

"Hey, I'm not completely sheltered!" she protested.

"Not completely..." he grinned, and she'd shoved him playfully.

"So you were drinking at that age, were you?" Lucy pressed Jeff.

"No, not me. But I guess some of the kids in my year did. You know I was a geek."

"You say that in the past tense?"

"Hey!" It was Jeff's turn to protest now, though he did so smilingly, and the twins smiled too.

The next morning, Maggie felt too nervous for breakfast, but Lucy insisted she at least have a piece of toast, with butter and marmalade.

Quite why she felt so nervous, Maggie had no idea. But she did have a crush on Robert Bastion, and she couldn't quite help imagining him asking her to dance. To what? Maybe *Don't Let the Sun Go Down on Me,* which was flying high in the charts. That was it. It would be the last dance – a slow one, and Robert would shyly ask Maggie if she'd like to dance to it. His friends might jeer, but he'd just ignore them, and he'd hold Maggie close as they swayed on the dancefloor.

In reality, there was nothing shy about Robert Bastion. He was one of those sporty, confident types, who was just the right side of cheeky to be able to get away with joking with the teachers, and he'd already had three girlfriends since the school year had begun. Nevertheless, Maggie was sure that he would be different with her, and she'd appeal to his romantic side. The lights from the disco ball spun around them as he put his arms around her...

"Come on, Maggie! We're going to be late." Julia shook her sister's shoulder gently. "Have you done your teeth?"

Lucy had left ten minutes earlier, for one of the primary schools, where she worked as the office manager. The girls always left the house last, and were usually home an hour or so before their mum. Jeff would be first out, leaving before eight, and last in, at around half past six. It felt as though they hadn't stopped since they'd moved down, and the stresses and strains of a new home, a new town, and new school or job had been taking their toll. They were all looking forward to some time off over Christmas.

"Yep, I'm ready," Maggie said, knowing full well that she hadn't brushed her teeth. Then, thinking of Robert Bastion, "Actually, just hang on a minute."

She rushed up to the bathroom, giving her face a once-over, smoothing down her hair, and chasing the toothpaste around her mouth with the brush.

"Come on!" Julia was practically glowing. Maggie knew that there was talk of Paul Cooper asking her sister out, at the disco. Julia was wearing her denim skirt and a sparkly top, and some soft grey boots that were an early Christmas present. Maggie was in jeans, with a long-sleeved t-shirt that had an image of a grizzly bear, in negative. She was wearing some skate shoes that her parents had also relented over, and given to her early. Sometimes she wished she was just a little more feminine, like her twin. Still, she was herself, and that was what was important. So her dad said, and so it was.

The girls left the house, into a day so warm and dry, it didn't seem possible that Christmas was just around the corner.

# Maggie

"I'll be down the week after next," Tony says, and I feel my heart do a little flip of joy. I'm lying on the sofa, while Stevie is fast asleep upstairs, and I have my phone balanced on my chest, set to speakerphone. "Though I wish I was here for your first day."

"Yeah," I say. "Me too." Then I think, no – honesty is the way forward. "Actually, I'm glad you won't be."

I'm gratified to hear his laugh – a burst of surprise. "Thanks very much!"

"No, you know what I mean. I need to start this job on my own terms. And I'm already really, really nervous. I think my stomach would be tied in knots if you were going to be there, too."

"I won't embarrass you," he says.

"Ha! No, I don't think you would. But I might embarrass myself. I'm a bit clumsy when I'm nervous. And I don't know what... how I should act around you. I mean, I know we've only really had one date, so it's not like..." I trail off. *Shut up, Maggie. Shut up!* goes the voice inside my head.

"I know what you mean," he says, reassuringly. I love the soft tone of his voice when we're speaking late in the evening. "And I know, it's weird for you. You're starting a new job, and you need to know you got it entirely on your own merits. And you are going to be

17

brilliant at it. At least we're working for different organisations. So it's not like we're colleagues or anything."

"But you were one of the people who interviewed me..."

"Well, yes, but that was just a formality. Graham had already decided you were the right fit. He just needed to feel like he's doing the right thing by his stakeholders."

*Stakeholders.* I don't feel like I'd ever really heard that word before the last two months, and then it was everywhere. I had genned up for my interview, and the presentation I had to give, and got to know a bit about Canyon Holdings, which is the company Tony works for, and which is financing the Saltings development and Saltings Social Enterprise, where I will be working. Graham will be my manager, and there are two support staff as well. It's nice to think we are all starting together. It's been hard enough trying to break into town life, without having to find my way in an established office environment, with all its in-jokes, and gossip, and politics. I really hope that we can start off positively and keep it that way. I've already met Amy, who is around my age, and Sheila, who is probably a good ten years older, although it's hard to tell. Amy lives in the next town, and her daughter will be going to the same secondary as Stevie, so we're planning to get them together over the summer if we can.

Oh, it's all so much to take in. A new job. A new man. A new school for Stevie. I regularly feel overwhelmed by it all. I might be standing at the sink, or pushing a trolley around the supermarket, when these thoughts come rushing over me, crashing like a wave on the rocks. How can I possibly manage it all? My instinct is to drop and hide, as I have been doing for a long time now. But that will get me nowhere, and, despite being terrifying, all of this is exciting. If I always pick the safe option; the one with the least risk, then I will carry on being bored – and very possibly boring.

"And am I allowed to see your posh office?" I ask now, smiling. The Saltings is huge; it encompasses a cinema, a surf school, bowling lanes, some community space, and some commercial properties – which are let to a coffee house and two restaurants, with offices above. I will be in an office on the first floor, while Tony's is one of the top floor suites. Once his job is done, overseeing completion of the whole development, the top floor will be up for lease to a different business. I don't like to think that far ahead.

I have barely known Tony any time, but I do like him a lot. And I know his job means moving about, sometimes internationally. So in twelve months' time or thereabouts, he may be sent elsewhere. Of course, we may no longer be seeing each other anyway by the time that happens, so I need to keep focused on the present. Enjoy things for what they are. It's just that it's been so long since I've had any kind of romantic relationship. I'm out of practice, and probably far too excited, and nervous, and sometimes verging on the neurotic. I feel a bit like a teenager again. But I am an adult and a parent, and I need to behave, and think, accordingly.

Alongside the Saltings commercial quarter are some residential properties, and it's these which have really set the cat among the pigeons as far as the locals are concerned. They've overshadowed some of the existing streets, and have stolen some of the harbourside views. I mean, this is not one of those picture-postcard Cornish harbours set in a little cove; it's more solid and industrial, and very much working. But the harbour is at the heart of the town, and so this big company coming in and essentially stamping all over it is understandably hard to accept.

And this is where Saltings Social Enterprise comes in. I really hope that it is more than just a nod to social responsibility. And not just to ease the way in for the Saltings, to then be knocked on the head and forgotten about. I can see great opportunities for the local community, but they need to be on our side, and open to fresh ideas.

"You are most certainly allowed to see my posh office," Tony says, his voice with a very slightly rough edge, which I love. He's so different to any of the men I've met this last decade or so. "We can watch the sunset together."

"I think it might be facing the wrong way for the sunset!"

"Oh. Damn. I have a lot to learn. How about the sunrise?"

"You should be able to see it from up there, yes. That would be an amazing thing to do."

"Does that mean we'll have to spend the night there, though?"

"Nope, just an early start!" I grin. I hope he knows I'm smiling.

"Shame."

"I know, I really hate early mornings."

"I meant it would be a shame not spending the night together."

"I know."

So this side of things is all very good. Since Stevie was born, I have had the odd date here and there, and I did actually have a short-lived fling with a wildlife photographer, one summer when Stevie was four. It was never going to be a long-term thing, but it was fun, and exciting, in a way that I've since almost given up on as a possibility.

I don't suppose living with Mum has helped, in some ways. She was always ready and willing to babysit, and I know she'd have liked me to be more sociable than I was, but staying with her was a safe haven, and Stevie a ready excuse not to go out, or make new friends, or form any kind of new relationship with a man. Plus, there was the problem of knowing most of the local men already, having gone to school with many of those who are my age, or them being parents of children at the school where I worked, or of Stevie's friends.

I had thought many times about moving on, but I never knew where I wanted to go, and I didn't want to leave Mum – or Julia, for that matter. It was circumstances which forced this change, and it's been hard. Tough for Stevie, who took a while to settle into her new school. She seemed to get on well with the boys and less with the girls, at first. But then she found her feet. And she does seem to love being right by the sea. Where we lived before, it was a ten-minute drive to the nearest beach. Which for some people is still a dream, of course, but it was always a bit of effort to do it and somehow, when you're in your weekly routine of school and work, and all the boring chores that come with those things, it can become hard to find the time and to make that effort. Now, we can just walk out of the house, down the road, and cross over near Elise's, down some steps, and we're on the sand.

Stevie is happier now than she was at first, and I think she is looking forward to secondary school. I remember being terrified of it, but then it was tied in with a move to a new place as well. She seems so much more confident than I ever was.

It will be a while before I introduce her to Tony, though. In fact, I can't believe that thought has even crossed my mind, really. I have met him in person literally three times. But we have spent hours and hours on the phone to each other, and I really feel like I know him. We have had one great date, when he took me to a lovely restaurant a bit further around the bay, and Elise had Stevie stay at hers. And, I confess, I had Tony stay at mine. I hadn't planned it that way; in fact, I'd been adamant that was one thing which wouldn't happen. But we had a lovely night. And it felt very natural. It was strange waking up with a man in my bed, though, and I felt slightly on edge, listening out for the sound of Stevie at the door, even though I knew that was unlikely. What would I have said, if she'd turned up unexpectedly?

Tony had seemed to sense my unease. "Shall we go out for breakfast?" he asked and, before I had a chance to answer, "Out of town, I mean?"

"I don't know. I would love to, but I'll have to go and get Stevie soon."

"No problem," he said, and kissed me, then sat up and swung his legs out of the bed. "I will get out of your hair, but don't think I'm running off, OK?"

"I don't," I smiled, then frowned. "But I don't want you to go, either."

"I know. I would love to stay, all day. Right here, in your bed, with you. But I know it's not as simple as that." He buttoned up his jeans, and pulled his shirt on. I took a last, longing look at his chest. "I'll head back to the hotel, for a shower, and I guess I'd really better get some work done anyway! You know where I am, for the next day or two, but I'll be back again in a couple of weeks, if I don't see you again this time. OK?"

"OK," I'd said. When I'd been out with Tony, and then when I'd invited him back to my house, I had felt like a completely different Maggie. A real, adult woman, with my own unique identity. It had been a long time since I'd felt that way. But with the new day, and the knowledge that I actually had an eleven-year-old daughter who I should really pick up from Elise's, the more usual Maggie started to seep back in. Maggie the mum. Maker of lunches and teas. Ironer of school uniforms. Story-reader. Rule-maker. Provider. Cuddler. Comforter. Worrier. The woman who in her late twenties had chosen to become a single mum, and never even told her daughter's father that was what he was. A woman with secrets, but a woman whose life revolves around her daughter, and who would do, and give up, anything, or anyone, for her.

# 1991

Lessons were pointless that day. The kids knew it. The teachers knew it. TVs and VCRs were wheeled into classrooms, in the hope of pacifying the unruly mob. The school thermostat was on a setting dictated by the time of year rather than the actual warmth of the day, and so classroom windows were slid open to let out some of the heat, and hopefully allow in some fresh air. The smell of thirty over-excited teens and pre-teens was a heady one: a strange and not necessarily pleasant combination of Impulse and Lynx body sprays.

By the end of the morning lessons, many of the teachers themselves had started to catch some of the feverish excitement, and were looking forward to the afternoon – not to the disco (never the disco) but to after the disco, with the promise of a cold beer, or a well-earned glass of wine, and the two weeks that lay ahead – days when it wouldn't matter if they stayed in pyjamas from morning till night. When there would be no Stephen Wilkins giving them cheek; no huddle of kids to chase from the corner of the school grounds where they gathered for not-so-crafty fags; and no planning. No marking. No children. Except for those with children of their own. Some of the younger teachers were in fact planning to return to their own parents, and siblings, and childhood bedrooms. Relaxing into the feeling of being somebody's child once more, rather than expected to be the grown-up in the room. The lines between adults and children began to blur, along with the line between what was acceptable school behaviour and what the kids could get away with.

Maggie, Julia and Stacey stuck together at break and lunch time. Stacey was wearing an outfit from Tammy Girl. A soft, white, long-sleeved top, which just skimmed her belly button, and some very light blue jeans. Maggie and Julia both felt slightly awed by how grown-up their friend was.

"You look great," Maggie said to her, always one to make other people feel good.

"Thanks, Maggie!" Stacey beamed. "You do, too," she added, apparently as an afterthought, and Maggie wasn't sure that she meant it. She felt young, and inconsequential, in comparison to her friend, and even her sister, and those dreams of Robert Bastion began to fade. She had seen him and his mates at the start of the day, and they had all but pushed past her, not even giving her a second glance, although she did wonder if Robert had perhaps manoeuvred closer to her, as his arm had definitely brushed against hers. Well, she was pretty sure it had. Time would tell, she thought.

"Who are you going to ask to dance, Stacey?" she asked. Stacey had been keeping her cards close to her chest. She had already gone out with two different boys, and one of them was a second year! Stacey had dumped them both, unceremoniously. Well, Julia had dumped them, on her friend's behalf. Maggie hadn't even been asked to carry out this dubious honour.

"I'm not asking anyone!" Stacey announced. "*They* will be asking *me*, or I'll be staying with my girls." She put an arm through one each of the twins', and together they walked to the hall for lunch.

The noise was close to deafening, and if the teachers had thought their stuffy classrooms were bad, they were nothing compared to the combination of smells in the hall. Gravy, mashed potato, greasy pizza, baked beans, turkey (it was Christmas, after all), mince pies and custard, mingling with the body sprays, and body odours, of the over-excited school population.

"Maggie, you grab those spaces over there, and we'll get your lunch," Stacey instructed.

Maggie followed Stacey's gaze. There were four spare seats at the end of one of the tables, two on either side. Right next to these empty seats was a bunch of fourth years. The sight terrified her.

"Go on," Stacey nudged her. Maggie wanted to tell her to do it, instead. What was she, Maggie, going to do if some older kids wanted their seats? She couldn't very well tell them they were taken. Stacey would. Julia might. But Maggie couldn't… could she? Nevertheless, she went obediently, and nervously spread her coat over two chairs, then sat in one opposite, at the very end of the table, putting her bag on the next seat. She felt hot and flustered, and had to sit on her hands to prevent herself from biting her nails. But nobody even seemed to notice her. And Julia sent her a smile and a thumbs-up from the dinner queue. It settled Maggie's nerves a bit. She just hoped she wouldn't be sitting on her own for long.

The fourth years were getting raucous, and one of the dinner supervisors was soon over to tell them to calm down, or they'd be straight outside; lunch or no lunch.

Maggie kept her head down, but listened to what the older kids had to say after the supervisor had moved along. Their language turned the air blue, Lucy would say. Maggie wondered if her mum and dad had any idea how different the secondary school world was to primary. The swearing. The rudeness to teachers, and each other. The fights! Maggie regularly wished she might be back in Bristol, at her safe little primary, where all the teachers knew her and Julia, and where she knew exactly where she was.

Stacey said she didn't miss Leeds at all. She hadn't been happy at school there, she said. And whereas the twins wrote letters to many of their old friends, and Lucy and Jeff were taking them back up there in the holiday for a big catch-up, and a night in a hotel, Stacey said she was OK with never going back to Leeds ever again. Neither Maggie nor Julia pressed her on this. They were both just glad that they had her now.

"Budge up!" Maggie felt an elbow in her back, and she froze, but then she heard the laughter.

"Stacey!" she laughed back, just relieved she wasn't about to become involved in some awkward situation.

"Soz," Stacey said, and she moved opposite Maggie, throwing her coat across the table. It fell on the floor and Maggie leaned down to retrieve it from amidst the squashed peas and carrots and lumps of cold potato left by previous diners.

Julia sat next to Stacey, and slid Maggie's lunch across to her. For all their differences, the girls had exactly the same taste in food, and Julia had chosen tuna mayo sandwiches, an orange juice, and a bowl of strawberry jelly for them both.

"Thank you," Maggie smiled at her sister.

"Don't look now," Stacey interjected, "but I think Paul Cooper's looking at you, Julia. *I said don't look!*" she hissed, as both twins turned to look in the same direction as their friend.

Paul Cooper was in the queue for lunch, and seemed pretty much preoccupied with his mates. Which included, Maggie noted, Robert Bastion. Not one of the boys was looking their way.

"Well, he was," Stacey shrugged. "Bet you get off with him at the disco, Julia."

"I don't think so." Julia looked uncomfortable at this prospect. Stacey had told the girls she'd kissed both the boys she'd been out with in Cornwall – and a couple of boys back in Leeds, as well. Neither Julia nor Maggie had kissed anyone yet, and neither really felt ready to.

"You say that now!" Stacey laughed.

Maggie shot her twin a small smile.

"What about you, Maggie? You still making eyes at Rob?" Stacey said, a little too loudly for Maggie's liking.

"Oh, erm, no. Not really." Since when did Stacey call him Rob, anyway? They were in the same home economics class, and had music together, too. Stacey said he was really funny. Maggie liked that idea, as long as he wasn't rude with it.

"No? Who is it, then? You going to ask anyone to dance? Or be a wallflower?"

"I'm like you, Stacey. If nobody asks, I'm not going to ask them," Maggie said, hoping she sounded more confident than she felt. "I'll stick with you and Julia."

"But what if we're both taken?" Stacey asked and Julia looked at her sharply.

"That's not going to happen," she said, her eyes on her twin.

"I'll be fine," Maggie said, not wanting anyone's sympathy. But it hadn't occurred to her that she might be left standing, while her sister and her friend were otherwise occupied. Her stomach began to hurt.

"I won't leave you anyway," Julia smiled, but her kindness just made Maggie feel worse.

Stacey, seemingly oblivious, asked, "You not finishing that sandwich, Maggie?"

"No, I'm full now." Her appetite all but gone, she pushed the plate across to her friend, and the jelly to her sister. Suddenly, she didn't want to go to the disco. She just wanted to go home.

# Maggie

**I just wanted to wish you well for today,** Mum's text reads. **And say that you will be brilliant. And I cannot wait to see you and my granddaughter next week! I love you. Xxx**

My mum. Always thoughtful. Always knows just what to say. She more than anyone will know that my stomach will currently be twisting itself into knots. That I am not as calm and confident as I try to make out. And that I am currently having major doubts as to whether I can really do this job.

It seems to have come round so fast, my first day. And it's coincided with Stevie's last week of school. Graham has said that I can have time off to go to her leavers' assembly, which is so nice. I'm going to be a mess. Even though she's only been at that school for a short time. It's more to do with her growing up, I suppose. It's incredible to think that we have reached this stage already.

But I can't even think about that right now, because my first major hurdle this week is to start my job. It's just a short walk from my house, which is a novelty in itself. When I lived in Bristol, I had to allow up to an hour to get to work, and then the same back home again. Now, I can see Stevie off, and then lock up and wander along towards the harbour. And today is an absolutely glorious day for it. The gulls are out in force, heralding my arrival (or, more likely, awaiting the return of the fishing fleet). I see a sleek seal's head break the surface of the dark waters, then it turns and gracefully returns to the depths, its long, shiny back curving and glistening in the sunshine before it is once more out of sight.

I feel nervous and conspicuous even just walking along the harbour, although it's a walk I might do on any other day. But I am dressed more smartly than I normally would be; a pair of wide-legged trousers, a short-sleeved top and a light cardigan, and an actual handbag. Shoes, instead of sandals or trainers. I feel business-like, and a little out of place.

Soon enough, I am at the door. I'm in agony, my stomach churning and my head pounding. I have some painkillers in my bag, and I think I may as well take some as soon as I can, to release this tight band of tension. My palms feel sweaty, too.

*Deep breath, Maggie.* Before I have time to think any further about it, I am opening the door, into the lobby of the main building. The smell of fresh coffee greets me, and I breathe it in. I could get used to this. Then I make my way up the stairs to the first floor, to the door marked 'Saltings Social'.

Here goes.

"Morning, Maggie!" smiles Sheila. "Isn't this exciting? I've been looking forward to it for weeks!"

"Morning," I smile, immediately put slightly more at ease by her warmth.

Sheila's desk is opposite Amy's, but Amy's chair is empty, though her cardigan's on the back of it.

"Amy's downstairs getting us coffee," Sheila says. "She remembered you like a latte."

"That is so nice! It's going to cripple me financially, having a coffee shop downstairs, if I'm not careful."

"Maybe we should just make it a Friday treat," she suggests.

"That sounds very sensible!"

"Hi, Maggie." Graham appears out of his office. I actually have my own office, next to his. I've never had my own office before. And while it might not have quite the same incredible, far-reaching views that Tony's has, the window overlooks the harbour, where I can watch the boats come and go, and I can't believe my luck, really.

"Morning, Graham."

My new boss is a good ten or more years older than me, with greying hair and a moustache. He's worked in various charities and not-for-profits for Cornwall, and has loads of experience, and great contacts. I think I will learn a lot from him.

"Amy's just getting us some first-day coffees," he says. "My treat. Then maybe we can have an hour or two in my office, to work out where to get started. Sheila, once Maggie and I have an idea of where we're going, we can have a team meeting this afternoon. How does that sound?"

"Sounds good to me, boss," Sheila grins.

"Less of the boss stuff, though! It's Graham, OK?"

"Whatever you say, boss."

I check Graham's reaction and I'm glad to see he's

smiling. Just for a moment, I relax and laugh, too. Then I remember what this is all about and the doubts come flooding back in. I really, really hope I don't mess this up.

The day flies by, and my painkillers only keep my headache at arm's length. There is so much to think about; from the procedures of the office – which Amy and Sheila are drafting, after our team discussion – to understanding funding, which seems incredibly complex and baffling, but which Graham assures me I will get my head around in time.

Thankfully, my role is more to do with the practical application of projects, rather than managing finances. And Graham and I have agreed where we should begin – with the community room at the Saltings, and a programme of events and regular users, like the foodbank and food-share schemes; a new playgroup; a local history group; business networks. The space we can offer is modern and warm and bright, and probably beats the church hall hands-down, but it won't do to put people's noses out of joint, and so we need to tread carefully.

"This must be an addition," Graham says. "We are not trying to usurp anyone, or anywhere."

"Of course," I say. "God, I know what people – particularly older people – round here think about this place. And I can't say it's favourable. They won't like the coffee shop, or restaurants. They see them as a threat to existing businesses."

"I get that. What we need to do is make them see that this place can only be good for local businesses. It will bring people into the town–"

"Which is not necessarily a good thing, in some people's books." I'm surprised how comfortable and confident I already feel talking to Graham. And he actually listens to me.

"I know. They'd like it left how it's always been. And they don't want their streets swarming with holidaymakers. Which is also fair enough. But I think the Saltings is going to be so good for the younger generation. And the not-so-young, as well. People still young enough to work, in short. There are jobs here, which weren't here before. And support for local groups, which means loads of different people are going to benefit. It's just a case of getting people to see that. It's not going to be easy, Maggie. Are you up for the challenge?"

"I am. I definitely am." And I realise that, more than being nervous now, I'm excited by it all: by my office, and my colleagues, and all the projects we're going to run. By the time the day is over, although my head is still pounding, and I feel utterly exhausted, I realise that I've been so caught up in my work I've barely thought about anything else. I walk out onto the harbourside and breathe in the strong, salty air, which has a slight tang from the day's catch. I feel like skipping, all of a sudden. I won't, of course – what if somebody saw me? But I have a sudden rush of energy and positivity, which I have not felt in a long while. I think, in fact, that I'd forgotten it is possible to feel like this.

I know some people here will hate whatever we do at work. All of this is unwanted change, and unnecessary, to their eyes – and I really, truly do sympathise. But it's happening – in fact, it's already happened, much of it. The major building work is done. The coffee shop is open, and it won't be long before the restaurants are, too. The offices around us are being leased, and will soon be filling up. The houses are being completed in the next few months. I feel like I am riding on the crest of a wave. I can't wait to see where it takes us.

# 1991

The sports hall was vast and cold, and really quite dark, with a corrugated roof, and breezeblock walls. Not your average Christmas disco location. Someone had rigged up spinning coloured lights around the walls, and Mr O'Connor was safely installed with his 'decks' at one end, behind a barricade of football nets. The equipment cupboard was bolted shut, and under the watchful eye of Miss Beulah, one of the girls' games teachers. The previous year's disco had seen a break-in to this cupboard by the fourth- and fifth-years, with dozens of netballs and basketballs sent bouncing across the dancefloor. The next thing, there had been a large-scale game of dodgeball taking place, with the balls far outweighing the dodges. There were bruised arms and legs, and even a black eye, and the head was called to give both years a dressing-down.

It had been suggested that the discos be called off, but the staff had relented, and so Maggie found herself trotting into the cool, loud hall, shepherded along with the rest of her form.

She looked around for Julia and Stacey – she would join up with them as soon as she could. She knew the other children in her form must think her quiet, but she hoped that she smiled enough to let them know she was not unfriendly. But the others seemed to all know each other from their primary schools, and it was hard to break in to their established friendships. Paul Cooper and Robert Bastion were in her form, so all was not lost. The only problem was, she sat at the front, and predictably they had taken seats at the back, so she could only really hear them, rather than see them (unless she turned round to stare, which really would not be the done thing). And she could always hear them – Robert, at least. He was loud and confident, and their form teacher, Miss Beardmore, seemed to like him. She accepted his cheeky charm with a smile. He always seemed to know just how far to push it.

Maggie sat by a boy called James Watson, who was slightly smaller than her, and nearly as quiet as she was. It seemed he'd been at primary school with Paul and Robert, so sometimes they'd come next to Maggie to talk to James. She always kept her head down, wishing she could think of something to say. Occasionally, she'd have an idea, but usually this was after they'd moved on to their own seats, and she would never have dared to speak up anyway.

Back in Bristol, at primary school, she'd never been bothered about putting her hand up. She had known every one of the other children, most of them from the age of four, and by and large they all got on well.

Looks had not been something she had given much thought to there, but here, in this secondary school world, they had taken on so much more importance. And not just people's faces, but their hair, their clothes… and their bodies. Maggie knew she was changing, and becoming curvier – much more so than her slender twin. It pained her, to think that other people might notice this about her. In fact, the whole scrutiny of people's appearances was painful to her.

"Looks aren't important," Lucy had said to her daughter, whilst looking in the mirror, applying her mascara.

"Then why are you wearing make-up?"

"Ha! You've got me there!"

"And why do you shave your legs and your armpits?"

"Oh... I don't know." Lucy looked thoughtful. "I just do. Always have. I like to wear make-up to work because it's a bit like putting on a face. A mask. It's part of my work persona. And you know I never wear it at home."

"So why at work, then?" Maggie had pressed.

"Again, love, I don't really know. It's just what I do. And as for the shaving... well, if I stopped now, I know I'd hate it. Fuzzy legs and hairy armpits. It's wrong, I know. Men don't feel the need to do it, after all. But it's just the way things are."

The way things are. That explanation was frustrating to Maggie. But she knew her mum was sensible. And so different to Stacey's mum, Sarah, who was immaculate, Lucy said (and it didn't exactly sound like a compliment). Her hair, her make-up, her clothes. Sarah was not working at the moment – "Between jobs!" she'd laughed – but she had worked up in Leeds, apparently. She'd had been at a public relations firm there. Stacey said that Sarah had worked with celebrity clients, but she wasn't allowed to *divulge* who they were.

Sarah was a mystical being, to the girls. Both Maggie and Julia were awed by her. And Maggie had to admit, she wouldn't mind looking like Sarah when she was older. Which cut straight through her principles, and made her feel bad for asking critical questions of her mum, but growing up was a complex business. Lucy herself said so.

Right now, Maggie was medium height, medium build. She had shoulder-length brown hair, and freckles. She had dimples, which she didn't like, and dark brown eyes. Like chocolate drops, Jeff said.

She knew she was not interesting to look at. And she dressed to confirm this. Almost as if challenging somebody to look beyond her clothes, and her looks, and find the real her. The important part. The person. She knew that was the key. Not how she looked, but who she was. The only problem was, nobody seemed particularly interested in looking any further.

And that strong resolve dropped away when it came to school, where she longed to fit in, and she both dreaded and desired being noticed. Now, as she scurried along with the others, she felt her form break away, as friends from other forms called to each other, and began to create little sub-groups.

Maggie looked around keenly again, for her sister and her friend. "Maggie!" she heard, and turned to see her sister waving. She smiled, flooded with relief, and hurried towards Julia, but stiffened as she saw that she was being beaten to it by Robert, and Paul, with James Watson following on. The boys reached Julia and Stacey before she did. Maggie could see Stacey smiling widely at them, while Julia had eyes only for her sister. But Stacey nudged Julia, and said something to Paul, then all but shoved them together. Maggie felt a rage bristle in her at this, but Julia didn't look like she minded too much.

Maggie reached them, and stood awkwardly.

"Hi, Maggie," said James.

"Hi." She looked past him, to Stacey, who was

whispering something to Robert. Was she telling him Maggie liked him? She wouldn't, would she?

"Oh hi, Maggie," Stacey said.

"Hi Stacey." She couldn't think of anything else to say. My god, was she really so boring? In that moment, she hated herself.

Some of the other boys from Robert's gang arrived, scuffling with each other good-naturedly, then a little gaggle of girls from Julia and Stacey's form tagged on to their group. Maggie shrank back even more. She wanted to talk to Julia, but her sister's attention was well and truly taken with Paul, and shortly he was pulling her gently to the dancefloor, to wolf-whistles and stamping of feet. Julia looked embarrassed but pleased, and Paul took her hands, so they could dance to Marky Mark and the Funky Bunch. Soon they were joined on the dancefloor, by a handful of other couples, and a few groups of girls who were dancing together.

The boys who did not have dance partners hared about the outskirts of the hall, skidding on the floors, and pushing each other good-naturedly towards the groups of girls who were still lining the walls

Maggie wanted to shrink back into those cold breezeblock walls. Without Julia by her side, she felt lost. And Stacey was busy laughing and joking with the other girls. Maggie watched her sister.

Paul was a bad dancer; that much was clear. And Julia was just sort of moving her feet, while Paul did a poor job of leading her. It was completely the wrong type of music to be dancing to in that way, anyway. And Julia knew so much about dance, and music. Yet she was hiding all that, and letting him lead. But she liked

Paul. Maggie knew that. And she might have been dancing badly, but she looked happy. Really happy. Her shining eyes caught the light, and Maggie felt at once happy for her sister, and envious.

It was only an hour, she told herself, but it seemed an incredibly long time. Julia and Paul returned, but they kept themselves to themselves. Maggie edged further into the main group, and tried to hear the conversation. She attempted smiling at the jokes she half-heard, but nothing felt natural.

By and by, the hour was drawing to a close. Maggie heard the opening notes of *Don't Let the Sun Go Down on Me*. This was it. The song she had envisioned dancing to with Robert. In her heart of hearts, she knew it wasn't going to happen now. He had barely glanced in her direction – if he had looked her way at all. But maybe, just maybe, he was as shy as she was. The dancefloor was filling up. Paul was whispering to Julia, and then the two of them headed towards the dancers, where he put his arms around her waist and she put her arms around his neck, and Maggie felt that same mix of emotions at the sight of them. Not long now, she told herself. Then this ordeal would be over. But then came the sucker punch. There was Stacey, with none other than Robert Bastion. The two of them tucked into the crowd of dancers, close to Julia and Paul. Robert pulled Stacey close to him, and she laid her head on his shoulder. She did not look at Maggie, and Maggie could not bear to look at her. Instead, she headed to the door, and asked Miss Hughes if she might be excused to go to the bathroom.

"But there's only four minutes left," Miss Hughes

smiled. "Are you sure you can't wait?"

"I think I've got my period, miss."

"Oh, OK. Go on, then. Don't forget to get your bag. And happy Christmas."

"And you, miss." Even upset, Maggie could not help but be polite. She ran towards the girls' toilets, and locked herself in a cubicle, sitting on the closed toilet seat, and feeling her eyes fill with tears.

After allowing herself a few moments' misery, not wanting to be discovered crying, she stepped back out and looked at her red eyes in the mirror. She scrubbed angrily at her face, then took a deep breath. And another.

Back in the corridor where the bags and coats had been piled, the space was already rammed with over-excited first-years, all ready to head home for the holidays. Outside, the second- and third-years were queuing for their turn in the sports hall disco.

Maggie saw Julia, who was now with Stacey. There was no sign of Paul, or of Robert. It seemed that once out of the dubious romance of the sports hall, they had reverted to form, and the girl-boy divide was strictly back in place.

"Maggie! I've got your coat!" said Julia, holding it out.

"Thanks. Have you seen my bag?" Without thinking, Maggie was acting like nothing was wrong.

"Erm, no, they're all a bit of a mess."

Grateful for a reason to busy herself, Maggie set to rummaging through the pile of bags until she found hers. She slung it over her shoulder. "Come on," she said to Julia, "Mum'll be waiting for us." She found she could not look at Stacey.

"OK!" Julia said, clearly still on cloud nine. "See you, Stacey!"

"Yeah, see you Christmas Eve."

Christmas Eve. The two families were meant to be getting together at the Patterns' house.

"See you, Maggie," Stacey called.

Maggie looked at her. Was that sympathy, or guilt, or even a glint in her eye? Or was Maggie imagining it? Stacy was her friend, after all. If Robert had asked her to dance, that wasn't her fault, was it?

"Bye, Stacey," Maggie said, her resolve crumbling. She was weak, she knew, but friends were more important than boyfriends. And besides, the two families were inextricably linked. She couldn't fall out with Stacey, even if she wanted to.

# Maggie

"So, who's looking after Stevie, again?"

I've already told Mum, more than once. It's because I haven't really mentioned Elise much to her before. It sounds silly, but I think I worried that she'd think I was replacing her.

"Elise," I say patiently. "A lady I got to know through that group where I volunteered."

"Well, isn't she a little old? Won't Stevie get bored?" I know Mum wants Stevie to come and stay with her at home for the first week of the summer holidays. In many ways, it would make sense. And I'd have a good chance to get really settled in at work. But I don't want Stevie away from me for a whole week. And I also want to be able to go to the beach with her in the evenings. I already feel bad enough for working through her school holiday. I also don't want her up there without me, as I know she'll see Julia – which is, of course, more than fine, but then what if Julia's seeing Stacey? I just can't let that happen. Maybe it's unrealistic to think we can avoid it forever, but I'm going to give it my best shot.

"No, Stevie really likes her. Plus Ada, Elise's granddaughter, will be there, and Stevie's really looking forward to meeting her. She's eighteen or nineteen, I think, so it's very exciting for Stevie. But we can't wait to see you, Mum. Stevie can't stop talking about it."

I need Mum to know I'm not cutting her out. She was hurt when we moved down here, though she tried her best not to show it. I suppose it was a bit of a shock to her. I'd been looking for a place of my own, as I should have done years before, and that was fine by Mum. But she'd thought we'd be staying close to her, and now we're a good hour-and-a-half away (or three hours on a bad day during holiday season).

"I can't wait to see her. Or you. I miss you both."

"I know, Mum." She's not trying to make me feel guilty, but I do. "We miss you, too. We're going to have so much fun this summer."

"I'm going to swim in the sea every day."

"Yes! You'll love just being able to walk down to the beach."

"I think I will."

"And Stevie can show you where there are some great little bays – you know, when I'm working. Then we can have barbecues on the beach in the evening, or take some sandwiches down."

"And have Film Fridays?" she suggests.

"Yes! We've missed those."

Every Friday when we were at Mum's, the three of us would have home-made (or sometimes takeaway) pizza and take it in turns to choose a film. Mum and I would share a bottle of wine, and Stevie would have a milkshake. Sometimes, Julia would join us. I miss those times. I'm really looking forward to having Mum close by, even if it's just for a few weeks. After the loneliness of the last winter, while Stevie and I still felt very new, and out of place, it's nice to know that the not-so-good times swing round again to better times.

And now really does feel like one of those better times.

I wonder if Elise thinks it strange that Mum's coming down. After all, I've given her the impression that we're not that close. Why wasn't I just honest from the start? But I know full well, there is never just one lie, or just one secret. To keep them viable, they have to be propped up by other falsehoods and dishonesties. I suppose I thought Elise must wonder why I hadn't stayed close to home, instead choosing to move to a little old town where Stevie and I knew nobody. It wasn't like work had brought me this way. But to tell her the real reason why I'd left would have meant revealing something I have never told anyone. I should have had it all straight in my head. It would have been so easy to say that I wanted to move closer to the sea, and that rental prices are much more reasonable here. Both of which things are true. But instead, on the spot, I concocted a story that I thought would explain why I had not stayed close to my family. I didn't look ahead, to a point where I might have to bear that reality out, or be revealed as a liar.

# 1991

On Christmas Eve, the Patterns had invited the Cavendishes to their house for 'drinks and nibbles'. Lucy had said she would drive, so that Jeff could have a drink. "You deserve one, you work so hard," she had said, in front of the girls.

"You work hard too, Mum!" Maggie had exclaimed.

"That's true, love," said Jeff, but Maggie noted that he didn't offer to drive instead.

"I'm not fussed about a drink anyway," Lucy continued. "I'll maybe have one when we get home. I don't want to be too late, mind."

"No, definitely not. We need these two tucked up in bed, safe and sound, before Santa gets here." Jeff peered at his daughters as he said this, to gauge their reaction, but neither objected to his statement, so it looked like it was to be another year of putting out the mince pie and whisky, and obligatory reindeers' carrot. "I hope he can find us in Cornwall," he pushed it just a little further.

"Of course he will, Jeff," Lucy scolded him. She too had a sneaky glance at the girls, but neither seemed to react in anyway but acceptance.

Just after lunch, they were ready to go – Lucy wearing her soft woollen jumper dress, which Julia coveted, and the girls in the same clothes they'd worn to the disco. Jeff had a new shirt on, and jeans. They piled into the car, singing along to the Christmas hits on the radio all the way. The Patterns lived in the next village, only ten minutes' drive away. They had a large house, the Old Rectory, on the outskirts of the village, and large gardens, behind tall old hedges.

"One day," Jeff said, as Lucy pulled the car into the drive. "Something like this… one day, eh?" He leaned across, and kissed Lucy on the cheek. The girls looked at each other and pulled faces, though both felt secretly pleased that their parents loved each other so much.

Sarah and Stacey were at the door in no time at all, with their little dog Juno in Sarah's arms, wriggling to be put down.

"Juno!" Maggie called, unable to help herself, and it was too much for him. He leapt from his owner's embrace, and was soon running across the gravel to Maggie, as fast as his little legs could carry him.

A dog was what Maggie wanted more than anything. In fact, it had been the only item on her Christmas list. She was more than envious of Stacey's collection of pets: not only Juno, but an older, bigger dog called Stan, as well as three guinea pigs called Milly, Molly and Mandy, and a rabbit called Bert. Maggie had put a note on her list that if she couldn't have a dog, then a guinea pig and/or a rabbit would make a nice consolation prize.

"I don't think Santa brings live animals, love," Jeff had said.

"Oh. Yes, I suppose you're right." She had added roller boots, Nirvana's *Nevermind* album on cassette – "Yes!" Jeff had exclaimed. "I'll have a copy of that, please." "If Santa gets it," Lucy reminded him. "Oh yes, that goes without saying, doesn't it?" – some Judy Blume books, watercolour paints, and watercolour paper. Maggie enjoyed drawing and painting, and was hoping she had inherited Lucy's artistic streak. She could just see herself setting up an easel by the beach, or up on the headland somewhere. The wind blowing her hair back off her face, her eyes trained on the view, and some passing walkers stopping to admire her artistic skills... She had added an easel to her list.

Now, she let Juno leap into her arms, and she held him close, laughing as his little hot tongue licked her face.

"Sorry about that!" Sarah called, stepping across to greet Lucy and Jeff with a kiss on each cheek. The girls knew Lucy hated this and thought it pretentious, but of course they never told Stacey so.

"Julia! Maggie!" Stacey called. "Come on, let's go up to my room!"

Maggie had put Juno down, and he ran around the grown-ups' ankles, desperate for somebody to give him some attention. Stan had trotted around the corner of the house, much calmer than his smaller counterpart, and had settled pretty much on Jeff's feet, leaning against his legs.

"He loves you, Jeff," Sarah said, ruffling the top of Stan's head then bending to scoop up Juno and, Maggie couldn't help but notice, revealing an awful lot of cleavage in the process.

"Hi girls," Rob, Stacey's dad, said, as he came down the stairs, and they brushed past him in their hurry to follow Stacey.

"Hi, Mr Pattern," Julia and Maggie chorused.

"Hey, it's Rob, OK?"

"Dad just wants to feel young," Stacey said.

"I heard that!" Rob said. "Cheeky."

"You were meant to hear it!" Stacey rolled her eyes at her friends. "Come on!"

Stacey's room was in the attic and both the twins coveted it enormously. She had been given free rein to decorate it as she liked, and consequently the walls were covered with posters, of popstars like George Michael, and Michael Jackson, with her developing taste starting to creep in, so that poster of the Cure's *Boys Don't Cry* sat next to a picture of Bros that had been ripped out of *Smash Hits* a year or two before, and a centre-spread of Corey Haim and Corey Feldman in *Lost Boys* partially obscured a picture of Scott and Charlene from *Neighbours*. One wall of Stacey's room was left uncovered by posters, and she was free to draw, paint, write, on this wall – "They want me to express myself. Well, Mum does, anyway," Stacey had said, the first time that the girls had been around.

"Wow!" Maggie was in awe of all this. She could not imagine her mum and dad letting her do anything like this in their neat, clean little house. They had wallpapered all the rooms when they'd moved in, and, although they had let the twins choose their wallpapers, and curtains (with some guidance), it still very much felt that the house was Jeff and Lucy's, and that they should have final say over anything that happened to it. In the Pattern household, Stacey had a lot more say, and sway, over what occurred. It sometimes seemed that she was treated more like an adult than a child.

Whenever they were over at the Patterns', Maggie liked to doodle on the wall, and Stacey had drawn a large circle, and written 'Maggie's space' at the top of it. "You can do whatever you like in this circle," she'd said, magnanimously.

"What? Really?" Maggie had exclaimed.

"Yes."

"Thank you so much, Stacey," Maggie had said, and Stacey had looked pleased, but had shrugged, as if to say it was nothing.

Now, Maggie sat by the wall, leaning against it, while Julia and Stacey sat on the bed.

"What happened with Paul, then?" Stacey asked.

"Nothing!" Julia blushed. "Well, nothing more than you saw. But he said he's got a Christmas present for me."

"I bet he has," Stacey said, which went over the girls' heads. "I wonder what it is," she quickly added, reading the room expertly. Sometimes, she felt so much older than her friends. But they were very sweet.

"He said his mum's going to let him drop it round, today."

"How exciting!" Stacey squealed. "I bet it's there when you get back home. Did you get him anything?"

"No, I... do you think I should have?"

"Well, dur! Although... it's good that he's putting in the work, and you're like, whatever."

"Oh no, it's not like that," Julia said, her face a picture of concern.

"Don't worry, Julia," Maggie spoke up. "You can see what he got you, and we're shopping at the sales in Bristol, remember? We can get him something then."

"Are you? Shopping?" Stacey asked.

"Yes, with Mum, and Dad. Though he'll get bored and go off for a coffee," said Julia.

"Or a beer!" Maggie grinned.

"Yeah," Julia smiled at her twin, "we always do it.

Well, we used to, when we lived in Bristol…"

Maggie couldn't wait to go shopping in Broadmead. They'd start at Debenhams, then move along to Etam, then C&A – usually by this point, Jeff had had enough, but he'd go good-naturedly off and they would meet a little later for lunch. When they lived there, at Christmastime they'd have got the bus into town, and they would spend all day there, so that they were still in the centre when the lights came on. Then, tired and happy, and laden down with bags, they'd get the bus back home, for a night in with pizza and a fashion show, Lucy and the girls parading their bargains in front of Jeff.

Now, it would be different. They would be staying with their dad's friend Simon and his family – which was ace because they hadn't seen Siobhan and Rory, Simon's kids, for ages. But they wouldn't be free to come and go as they pleased, and they couldn't very well have a fashion show at somebody else's house, or even choose what they had for tea. Maggie thought longingly of their house in Bristol, which Jeff and Lucy had moved to when Lucy was pregnant, and where the twins had been brought back as newborns… and where their parents had held a little wedding reception for themselves, when they'd finally got married, when the girls were three years old.

Maggie knew all the night-time noises of that house, and the street. In a close-knit terrace, where they could hear their neighbours either side of them. It felt so safe and secure, and snug. Here, it was different. Everything was. And, looking at Stacey and Julia sitting on the bed, while she rested her back against the cold wall, she felt her stomach ache with a longing to feel that familiarity once again. She felt cast adrift.

"So, what about you and Robert?" she found herself saying to Stacey, with a challenging note in her voice.

Stacey looked surprised, and innocent. Maggie could tell it was put on, and probably well-rehearsed. "Oh, you mean, when we danced? Oh, well, it was just the end of the disco, wasn't it, and everyone else was dancing. There was nothing in it, Maggie. You should have asked him, if you wanted to dance with him."

"You mean *you* asked *him*?" Julia looked shocked.

"No, no," Stacey quickly answered, her broad West Yorkshire accent coming on strong. "No, he asked me. Well, I don't know. We ended up dancing together. It doesn't really matter, does it? Anyway, what about James? I reckon he likes you, Maggie."

"Oh yes, he does, Maggie," Julia said earnestly. "Paul told me. James wanted to ask you to dance, but he was way too shy."

James Watson. Maggie thought of her neighbour in her form room. A nice boy. But she didn't fancy him. What would she have said, if he had asked her to dance? She couldn't have said no, could she?

"It's true, Mags," Stacey slid in with her abbreviation of Maggie's name. Nobody else called Maggie that. Her real name was Margaret, after Lucy's mum, but nobody had ever called her that, either. Not even when she was a baby. She had always been Maggie. "He really likes you. I'd forget Rob anyway, James is more your type."

Was he? Maggie had wondered. Could she like James? It was only later, on the way home, that she realised Stacey had cleverly put an end to the topic of herself and Robert Bastion. And what did she mean, James was more Maggie's 'type'? But by then, the girls had enjoyed themselves so much, it no longer seemed to matter.

They had joined the adults for board games, and the so-called 'nibbles', which were an endless stream of crisps and nuts and olives and canapes, provided by Sarah, who also kept Jeff's glass topped up, and her own, and sometimes Rob's, while occasionally remembering to offer Lucy a drink – as though, because she wasn't drinking alcohol, there wasn't really any point offering her anything. They had filled up on all the savouries, but then came mince pies, and shortbreads, and chocolate tarts – although Sarah seemed to be pronouncing them 'torts', to Maggie's ear; perhaps it was her accent – and a huge box of Thornton's.

"We won't need to eat anything tonight!" Lucy had laughed. "Thank you, Sarah."

"Oh, you can stay for dinner too, if you like," Sarah had said. "Why don't you?"

"No, no, that's very kind of you, thanks," said Lucy. "But we've lots to do." She looked at Jeff, who took the hint.

"That's right. We've got to put out the mince pie for Santa too, haven't we, girls?"

"Do you still do that?" Stacey asked, as though incredulous.

"We haven't done that for years, have we?" Sarah said. "Not since we told her Santa doesn't exist."

A hush fell on the room. Lucy and Jeff looked at their daughters, who looked back at them.

Rob kicked his wife under the table.

"Ow! What was that for?"

"Course he exists!" Rob laughed smoothly. "Sorry, girls, she's had a couple too many…"

"I hav… oh, yeah, sorry. I think this wine's gone to my head! Silly me. As if Santa doesn't exist."

Well, Julia and Maggie had discussed this between themselves more than once. But they'd agreed to keep quiet about it when it came to their parents, and 'suspend their disbelief', as they'd been learning about in English. It was too late now, though. The cat was truly out of the bag. And shortly afterwards, the Cavendishes left the Patterns to their Christmas (which included quite a hangover for Sarah) and went on their way to their new home, and a new reality, where the girls felt just a little bit less like children.

"So, can I have a dog?" Maggie asked, breaking the silence in the car on the way home. It made everyone laugh.

"We'll see," said Lucy, and Maggie beamed at Julia. They both knew what that meant.

# Maggie

For quite a long time, I felt like life was too quiet. Too predictable. When we'd moved down here – a major change – I realised that life actually became even quieter, and even more predictable. For the first few months, it was all about Stevie. And I liked being able to focus on her in a way I hadn't for some time. I could walk her to and from school. We could go to the beach on our way home, or later in the evening. I didn't have to worry about my own work; just her homework. But I knew it wouldn't be enough forever. So I started volunteering at Caring the Community, and I bought a car – the same model I'd had more than ten years before, after Dad had died. It's even the same colour. Back when I'd bought the first one, it had been nearly new and smart. This second one is old but reliable, and worth a lot less than I paid the first time round. But it gave me some freedom and independence. And Stevie and I were able to go for days out, sometimes taking Elise with us, and the occasional trip back home. I had to plan these carefully, trying to ensure that there would not be a chance of bumping into Stacey while I was back.

I would ask Julia what her plans were for the weekend. I know she and Stacey had picked their friendship back up and were seeing quite a lot of each other.

"It's all about the school this weekend," she might say. Julia has her own dance school, and she's incredibly good at what she does. Her classes always have waiting lists.

"Any nights out planned?"

"No, not this weekend. But next weekend we're having a little get together of the old gang, just at the Feathers. Do you think you could come then? James will be there, with his girlfriend – you'll really like Tara, she's lovely – and Stacey, of course. She'd love to see you. I think she's up at her in-laws' this weekend, though. I'll check."

"Ah, that's a shame. I don't think I can do next week, though. I'm pretty sure Stevie's got a party to go to."

I don't ever like lying to my sister, but I feel like each of these little lies was just stacking up on top of the larger ones. And besides, it's quite possible she's been holding back the truth from me all these years, and I am sure Mum must have been as well. Over time, I've come to think that everyone has their secrets, and maybe that's OK. In our case – my mum's, my sister's and mine – we'll have been trying to protect each other. And ourselves, too; at least in my case. The question is, can we maintain this delicate balance forever? While secrets exist, there is always the possibility for them to come tumbling out, some time. And it's never possible to completely relax.

It has worked, though, and Stevie and I have had a few weekends back home, with Mum, Julia and Paul, without having to see anybody else from our past. It's not easy, and when we've had to leave, I've felt a real pang, from the separation, and worrying about Mum being on her own. But she has Julia. And Paul. And they have their friends, and their work, and Paul's family, too. And Mum has lots going on socially, and is still working, so I know she's OK, really. It's me that's missing out. Me and Stevie.

But now, life is changing, and it feels like a snowball rolling downhill. Gaining momentum. It's not uncontrollable, but it is picking up speed, and it's becoming hard work trying to steer it.

I pass Elise's house on the way up to the school. After coming into work early this morning, which Graham said I had absolutely no need to do, I left just before lunchtime, grabbed a bite to eat at home, and got changed, ready for the leavers' assembly. The Mums WhatsApp group was pinging non-stop with exclamations of sorrow, and reminders to bring plenty of tissues. There is a disco for the kids at the end of the school day, and parents have been told they can stay on for a drink on the school field while the kids party away.

Elise waves at me from her window. I remember when we used to pass her by, before I knew her. She'd often be sitting there, and I would try not to let her know I'd noticed. It must be hard, getting older, looking out at the world, and perhaps feeling less connected with it than you used to be. Seeing her there was one of the reasons I chose to get involved with the seniors' club, though I could never tell her that. She'd hate to think I'd noticed her loneliness. She's actually an inspiration, but again I could never tell her that, for fear of sounding patronising. Elise is a proud woman, and rightly so.

By the time I've reached the top of the hill, I've been joined by Sam, one of the other mums, and we're both hot and sweaty. "Blimey!" she says, "I don't remember it being this hard work when I went here."

Like a lot of the parents, Sam grew up here, went away to uni and work, and eventually found her way back, when she and her husband Andy became parents. Their son Toby was one of Maggie's first good friends at the school, and he'll be getting the bus with Stevie to secondary. I'm pleased. I always feel like he'd stick up for her, if she needed it. I am sure she would tell me it won't be necessary.

I remember being really shy of Sam at first. She is outgoing and bubbly, and into everything to do with the school – the friends' committee, school trips, the Christmas Fayre. But she's been really friendly to me, and helped me find my way into the throng of parents who gather by the gates at the end of the day.

We stop and take a moment to get our breath back, our faces turned to the sun and the sea. "What a place for a school!" I say. "What a view!"

"I know. Never appreciated it when I was a kid. But now…"

The water sparkles for miles and, far out, a tanker makes slow progress across the horizon. A gull swoops down before us, hanging in the air for a moment, before dropping down further towards town.

"Come on," Sam says. "Let's see if we can get a good seat!"

More parents and grandparents are milling about. The usual suspects have got here first, and already nabbed the front row. I'm surprised they haven't got a 'reserved' sign there. But Sam and I manage to find two chairs together at the end of the third row and, as I settle down, smiling at some of the others, I am hit by the enormity of the occasion. I mean, in years to come, this will be nothing, I know. Stevie will leave secondary school, maybe college and uni. She'll have jobs, I hope. A career. Maybe become a mum herself. Primary school will pale into insignificance. But right now, this is important.

Oh god. I think I'm going to cry. And the kids haven't even put in an appearance yet. On the screen at the front of the school hall are pictures of this lovely class of children, from reception all the way through to year six. How is it possible that they were ever so small? Stevie only makes an appearance late on, but when I see her smiling face, laughing with classmates, or her head bent over a piece of work, I can't believe how much she has changed, even over such a short space of time.

The class come walking proudly in, so grown up, and I watch them all as they make their way to the front benches, where, once they are all in line, they greet us, and then sit, facing us. Some are waving and grinning at parents, some are fidgeting, and more than one is looking anxiously around. But every child has at least one adult here for them. I look steadily at Stevie until her eyes rest on me, and she smiles. She mustn't see I'm blubbing! I take a slow, steady breath, and push my shoulders back. I'll be strong, for her.

It's not that easy, though, but I'm happy to say it isn't just me. The children do readings of poems they've written, and Stevie participates in a short play that she and three of the other girls have written, about starting at their new school. Playing the part of a less-than-bright teacher, she makes the audience laugh, and I swell with pride.

The afternoon is rounded off with award-giving, and there is something for everyone. Stevie is 'Most likely to be a stand-up comedian'. The audience cheer and whistle every one of the children and by the time they stand to sing their leaving song – the Lightning Seeds' *The Life of Riley* – there is not a dry eye in the house. Most of the children are crying, too. It is a relief to get outside into the fresh air. The kids come out too, for photos, and to hug their parents, and each other, then they are whisked back into the school hall, which has been deftly cleared by staff, for their disco, while us adults stand around, or sit on the grass, and sip Pimm's and lemonade from little white plastic cups.

When Stevie first started here, I was more nervous than she was, and felt so self-conscious, coming in and out of the playground. There was many a cold, windy, rainy day when I pulled my hood up and felt close to tears, though for no particular reason. I am gratified now to realise that I seem to be part of the scenery, and most people know me by name, and vice versa. When it's time to go, Mrs Wilkinson, the year six teacher, gathers us all together for a huge photo, of adults and kids alike. It is mayhem, but she takes a few shots, and promises to send them to us. No doubt in time that photo too will fade in significance, but I would like to think that I will remember this day forever.

"Can I go back to Jade's, Mum?" Stevie asks. "Hannah's going, too. For pizza and a sleepover. Her mum says I'm welcome to join them."

I look at Jade's mum, Mel. She nods her head. "Fine by me. It will be nice for them to keep on partying! As long as you don't mind, Maggie."

"Well, if you're sure, yes of course," I smile. "Shall I drop some things round?"

"Oh, would you, Mum? Thank you!" And Stevie runs off excitedly with her friends, while Mel and her partner Alan follow on behind.

So I make my way home alone, back down to our little house, and I open the door into the quiet. I would usually be grateful for an evening to myself, but I'd pictured Stevie and me celebrating together today. After all, it's a big day for me as well. I have somehow managed to get my daughter to this point, and she is happy, and doing well at school, and clearly good at making friends as well.

Still, this is how it is going to be, more and more, as she grows up, so I may as well get used to it. I gather her pyjamas, and some clothes for tomorrow, and wander round to Jade's house. There are shrieks of laughter from upstairs, and I can't help but smile. If Stevie is happy, then I am. Mel invites me in, for a glass of wine.

"I won't today, thanks, Mel. I'm shattered after my first week at work! But I hope you all have a great evening."

I walk away into the warm twilight and decide to take a walk by the harbour. I pass the office building, and go as far as I can, towards the harbour wall. I stop for a while there, resting on the old stone, imagining how many generations of people have done the same before me. The longer I look across the sea, the more details I pick out; patches of lighter water, and a clutch of gulls gathering behind a boat that is steadily chugging back towards shore. A small group of unidentifiable birds flies low above the waves, following a straight, unseen line to wherever their destination may be.

Turning back, I stop at the Co-op on the way home, and get myself a mini bottle of prosecco and a large bar of Dairy Milk. Although I don't often like to congratulate myself, it's been a big week, and, as Elise has told me, it's important to acknowledge our achievements.

# 1992

The first summer in Cornwall was the turning point, when Maggie realised that actually, although she still missed Bristol, and city life, the benefits of living by the sea were many. On hot, sultry days, when the school term was still running – children (and teachers) spent their days looking longingly out of windows, while the gulls soared high above, or sat on the roof, calling out to each other, and rubbing it in to the humans stuck inside the sweltering classrooms. *We're free, we're free!* – the girls would sometimes get home, loosening their ties and casting their bags to the floor as they entered the house, to find Lucy home early with the car packed, ready for an evening picnic and swim. Jeff would come to meet them at the beach, which would be scattered with like-minded families. It was something they could not have dreamed of before, and definitely made living in Cornwall more bearable.

Sometimes, Jeff would have invited the Patterns to join them. Sarah and Stacey and Juno would announce their arrival with shouts and waves (the Patterns' other dog, Stan, would usually stay at home, not being a fan of the beach, and tending to bark non-stop at the sea). Stacey and Juno would run down the dunes, while Sarah, normally dressed in something white and flowing, and a large straw sunhat, picked her way down more steadily. Jeff and Rob would join the girls in the water as soon as they were able to. They would swim and mess about in the sea for ages, with Juno watching from the shore, running back and forth and occasionally braving the very shallowest of waters, wanting to join in, but not quite daring to broach the waves.

The feeling of freedom was enormous and eye-opening. They often would not leave the beach until after nine, getting home to shower the sand off their increasingly tanned skin, and climbing into bed happy and exhausted in that unique post-beach way.

Once, they had been strict in their routines. Bed at eight, lights out at half-past. Jeff and Lucy were not tyrants by any means, but they had both felt the need to manage their days, and really insisted on at least an hour – hopefully two – to themselves at the end of each day. Now, the girls were older and more self-sufficient, but also their parents seemed less laced-up. More able to go with the flow, and enjoy each day as it came.

There were things they had to do, of course. Go to work, go to school. But everything else fitted in around it, and Lucy in particular felt liberated by discovering that life worked this way. Things still happened. She and Jeff were each earning a wage. Maybe not a huge wage, but enough to pay for their mortgage, and to keep them fed and clothed, with a bit to spare for the odd treat here and there. The girls were being educated, and had settled well at school. It felt like they were living at last.

The only downside, Lucy was finding, was that sometimes Jeff seemed less happy than her with the fact that they weren't better off, financially. She supposed it wasn't helped by the amount of time they spent with the Patterns, who were certainly wealthier than them, by a long way. Even with only one wage coming in. And Rob being Jeff's boss only made that more awkward at times. She knew that Jeff didn't always rate Rob very highly in terms of work. "He nearly made a total balls-up today, with the Sheffield order. And it's one that we do every two months. Good job Phil was there, and saw what was happening. Maybe I should have talked myself up a bit more, like Rob does. I could have had his job, instead."

"But we're fine as we are, aren't we?" Lucy would say. "We've got everything we need. The girls are happy at school, and I like my job. Also, you haven't got the same weight of responsibility he's got. Which I think is a good thing. We've got a nice house, with a lovely garden and great neighbours, and we can go to the beach every day if we want to! Isn't this everything we wanted, when we decided to move here?"

"I guess," Jeff would say. Then he'd put his arm round her, and kiss her. "Yes, you're right. As usual. But still, it's frustrating."

"I know," Lucy would soothe, "but also, they're our friends, aren't they? And he's Stacey's dad. And Sarah's husband."

In actual fact, Lucy wasn't one hundred per cent sold on Sarah – or Stacey, for that matter. It felt like there was an edge there, sometimes. Something to do with money, or appearances, or status. They were a bit loud and a bit brash, and not shy in talking about money. How much they had; how much their house had cost; the new kitchen, new car, etc. It didn't sit well with Lucy, who had been brought up not to talk about these things. Not because it was something to be ashamed of, but you never knew what struggles other people might be having, and besides, it was one of the least important aspects of a person.

There was something about Sarah not working, too. Lucy knew it was a choice, and Rob's salary was probably twice what Jeff earned, but it felt like Sarah was a Lady Who Lunches, and no matter how hard Lucy tried to find solidarity for all women's choices, she found it hard to respect somebody young, intelligent, and more than able to work, who chose not to.

She had ventured this thought, tentatively, to Jeff, but he had stood up for Sarah: "She's just a northern lass, isn't she? Down-to-earth. Straightforward. I don't think she's showing off, I just think she's being honest. And so what if she doesn't work? Rob's earning enough – more than enough," he'd added grudgingly.

It irritated Lucy that he thought Sarah was fine as she was. While she, Lucy, was working away, and trying to keep everything going for their two girls. She had no idea how Sarah filled her time – it wasn't like she even looked after the dogs. Lucy knew that Sarah employed a dog-walker, and even paid the neighbours' teenage son to clean out the rabbit and guinea pig cages. If she tried this approach to life, Lucy didn't think it would go down very well with Jeff. Still, she tried to let it slide. She did find Sarah good fun, and lively company, and while the girls were great friends with Stacey, and Jeff working with Rob, it was important to keep the friendship alive.

Still, she was pleased if one of the girls was invited to a different friend's house, or if they asked to have someone other than Stacey over sometimes. With their birthday coming up, towards the end of term, Lucy sensed the perfect opportunity to broaden their friendship group a little further, with a garden party/camp-out for the girls. She would let them choose two friends each – in addition to Stacey, of course – and invite parents to stop for a drink and a chat when they dropped the kids off.

The girls loved the idea, and chatted eagerly about it over dinner. "Who are you going to invite, Maggie?" Julia asked.

"Claire and Ellie, definitely," Maggie said without a moment's hesitation. Both these girls were in her form, and had come from the same primary school. They had gradually opened their friendship to include Maggie, who knew that they were best friends, but was grateful that they also included her in their conversations and sometimes invited her to eat lunch with them, although she would always sit with Julia and Stacey. Sometimes, they would all sit together. She didn't think Claire and Ellie thought much of Stacey, though, and it could be quite stressful trying to get them all to mesh together.

"What about you? Are you inviting Paul?" Maggie grinned slyly at Julia.

"No boys!" Jeff said, good-naturedly. "And how is Paul, these days?"

Julia shot her sister a look. *Thanks very much.* "He's fine, I think."

"You think, do you? Don't sound very sure!"

Julia and Paul's relationship, if it could be called that, had not really taken off. He still liked her, though, and she still liked him. His Christmas present had indeed been waiting when they got back from the Patterns that Christmas Eve, and Julia had shyly taken it to her room to open. Later, she had shown

Maggie the cuddly teddy holding a heart. Maggie knew Julia slept with it every night, then hid it behind some books on her shelf in the morning, hoping her parents wouldn't see it (Lucy had of course found it months ago, smiling to herself and saying nothing, not even to Jeff).

Maggie and Julia had both been invited to Paul's bowling party when he had turned twelve in April, and Maggie had won against all of them, including Robert Bastion. She'd glowed when he'd complimented her – "You're as good as any boy!" – but at McDonald's he'd pushed James Watson to sit next to her, and barely looked in her direction again. Meanwhile, Julia and Paul had sat shyly next to each other, barely speaking. It was definitely a slow-burner.

"Stop it, Jeff!" Lucy said now. "Leave the girl alone. Who are you going to invite, Julia?"

"I'm thinking Marie and Jackie," Julia said gratefully.

"Lovely. That sounds like a nice lot of girls. We can set up the tent for you all. That way if it's raining, you've got some shelter. If the others can bring sleeping bags if they've got them, we should have enough roll mats and camp beds. And we can rent a couple of videos, get some pizza and crisps…"

"And I'll head off down the pub!" said Jeff.

"You can if you like. You'll only be in the way," Lucy grinned.

"Thanks very much!"

When the day of the party finally came around, they were well into a run of perfect Cornish summer weather, and so they needn't have worried about needing shelter. They lifted the doors of the tent at both ends; otherwise, it was far too hot in there.

"Do we do balloons?" Lucy had asked. "Or are you too old for balloons?"

"I like balloons," said Maggie. "What do you think, Julia?"

"Yeah! Let's have balloons."

"Why not? You only turn twelve once."

While Lucy was blowing up the balloons, with the help of a pump, Jeff came downstairs. "Love, I am really sorry, but I'm going to have to go into work later."

"What?" Lucy looked up, red-faced from her exertions.

"You know Rob's away in Germany? Well, Alex's wife has gone into labour, and they need somebody to cover him."

"Oh, Daddy!" Maggie said. She had wanted Jeff to be there today. He was always good fun when they had friends over.

"Sorry, my love. It can't be helped." He kissed both the girls, and then his wife. "I am really sorry. But I'm here now. I don't have to go in till this afternoon. So what can I do?"

"You can finish blowing up these balloons," Lucy said. "I'm going to put the kettle on."

"OK!" Jeff said, grinning sheepishly at the girls. "I'll have them done in no time."

Mid-afternoon, Jeff headed off to work, and the party guests began to arrive. Lucy offered drinks to the other parents, but all politely declined, being either keen to make the most of their child-free time, or else having other children to ferry about as well. Sarah and Stacey were last to arrive.

"Do you want a cuppa?" Lucy asked Sarah, and was surprised when she said no.

"Sorry, love, I'm going to make the most of an afternoon off, and go shopping."

"That sounds nice," Lucy said politely, secretly pleased; she saw enough of Sarah as it was. It was the other parents she had been hoping to get to know a bit better.

"Yeah, and I'm getting my hair done later, too."

"Well, enjoy yourself," said Lucy.

"Thanks, I will." Sarah kissed Lucy on both cheeks, leaving a trace of her strong perfume on the air.

Lucy waved Sarah off, then turned to the girls. "Right then, it looks like it's just me and you girls. Why don't you get your beds set up for later, and I'll fetch you some drinks and snacks."

The seven girls headed happily into the garden, their laughter and chatter making Lucy smile. She filled up jugs with ice and home-made lemonade, and tipped party rings, salt-and-vinegar chipsticks and cheesy puffs into bowls. She knew it was the last year her girls were likely to entertain the idea of anything like a proper children's party, and the thought made her a little bit sad. Even though in reality they were normally hectic and noisy and stressful affairs, they were also times that she remembered fondly. Marking each year of her daughters' lives. There would be no party games this time, of course, but that wasn't too much of a loss. They always ended in tears, anyway.

Lucy kept back a few snacks for herself as well, realising that, with Jeff out, and the girls happily busy with their friends, she in effect had the afternoon to herself. She could hole up in the lounge with her book and a cold drink, and a bowl of crisps, and hope for at least half an hour's peace and quiet. Maybe it wasn't so bad that Jeff had been called into work.

The next morning, the girls were, predictably, shattered. Lucy had been out to them during the night to ask them to keep the noise down, for fear of upsetting the neighbours, and also so that she and Jeff could get some sleep. He had come back late from work, tired but surprisingly cheery.

"How's it gone?" he'd asked Lucy, kissing her cheek and peering into the near-dark garden, where the tent was illuminated with torches, the girls inside silhouetted on the canvas.

"It's been fine!" she smiled. "To be honest, it's been really easy. They have not stopped eating, and they've watched both the videos, and want to watch one again in the morning! And they've been in the tent ever since. I was hoping they'd be tired by now, but, as you can see…" she laughed.

The twins' friends were lovely, and Lucy had really enjoyed chatting with them all, and seeing her daughters so happy. She'd worried immensely about uprooting them for this move, but it just went to show that they were adaptable and friendly, and maybe it had been good for them. Pushed them to be more gregarious. Stacey had been nice, too, and seemed a little easier to take when she was diluted by a larger group. Lucy always felt a bit bad that she didn't like Stacey more, but maybe it was just those similar traits to Sarah's – the loudness and lack of inhibition – that grated. That day, though, she'd been much calmer, and Lucy had given her a hug when she'd come in to use the toilet. Stacey had looked pleased.

"Are you having a good time?" Lucy had asked.

"Really, yes, thank you," Stacey had beamed, and had looked her age for once.

"Well, I'm glad. And I'm glad the twins are friends with you." She had meant it.

"I'm sorry I had to go out," Jeff said, pulling his wife to him and kissing the top of her head. "I am really sorry."

"Don't sweat it. Honestly, it's fine. Now, if the girls were five, and you'd left me to do a party on my own, well, that would be a whole different matter!"

"I suppose they don't need us as much anymore," he said into her hair, slightly sadly.

"Don't you believe it," Lucy had said, pulling back and looking her husband in the eye. "They need us more than ever. Just in a different way."

They had left the back door unlocked, and Lucy had not slept much at all – even once all was quiet outside, she'd got up sporadically, to peer out of the window, hit suddenly by the responsibility of having seven pre-teen girls sleeping in her garden. Each time she'd looked out, the scene had been peaceful and quiet, and she'd enjoyed seeing the world come to life gradually, with the early-morning bird visitors, and the flowers beginning to glow in the growing sunlight. It had made her heart swell. That was the only way she could think of it. She was in Cornwall, with her family, and the girls were down there, sleeping soundly amidst their friends.

Unbeknown to the girls, on their actual birthday, the four of them were going to a nearby farm to collect their very own puppy. She knew Julia would be pleased, but for Maggie in particular it would be a dream come true. The summer holidays began on Friday, and although they couldn't afford a holiday away this year, why would they want to be anywhere else, anyway? They had all that they needed, right here.

# Maggie

Already it is week two of my new job, and week one of the school summer holidays.

"Are you sure you don't mind, Stevie?" I ask for the millionth time, although what would I do if she did mind? It's not like I can just stop going to work for a few weeks. And the truth is, she's super excited to be spending time with Elise and Ada. Realistically, it's Ada who is the draw for my daughter. A beautiful, free spirited young woman, who seems to know just how to talk to my eleven-year-old. I suppose, even though I think I remember it so well, it's been a lot longer for me since I was that age. And times have changed, too. People say kids are growing up faster these days. I don't know if that's true, but they are almost certainly growing up differently. And life for Stevie is different to how it was for me anyway. I had a dad and a sister, as well as a mum. I knew both sets of my grandparents, and I knew where I came from.

I suppose that's something that Ada and Stevie – and Elise, come to think of it – have in common. No dad. No known dad, anyway. Elise's died when she was too young to remember. Ada's dad is a mystery, apparently. Louisa, Elise's daughter, decided she wanted a child, and so she got one. She is very much a go-getter. A very successful career woman, who definitely knows her own mind. She, like me, opted out of relationships while her daughter was growing up, although I understand she's recently met and been disappointed by somebody she liked quite a lot.

I think that I'm a little bit scared of Louisa. She came to stay with Elise a few months ago, and I was due to take Elise out on the day that Louisa was leaving. I got to the house before she'd gone and I said hello, but then went to wait for Elise in the car. I know it looked like I was being thoughtful to the two of them, but actually I don't think I knew what to say. And I was worried she'll think I'm trying to take advantage of her mum in some way. I don't really like the 'alpha' label, but I am a wimp when it comes to people like Louisa, who probably has more in common with Stacey. I fear being made a fool of, and so I clam up, which I know makes me look even more stupid, but I get a dry mouth, and can't think of a thing to say.

Anyway, Ada clearly 'gets' Stevie, and Stevie clearly reveres Ada. We spent Sunday afternoon out at one of the local beaches – a small, sheltered, stony bay, which was not too busy, and Ada had Stevie in the sea immediately. It was a sweltering day, and I longed to be in the water myself, but it would have meant leaving Elise alone. Instead, she and I perched on the concrete wall that backed the beach, and watched the two girls, who seemed to hit it off immediately, laughing and splashing each other, and taking the plunge for a swim.

"Ada's lovely," I said to Elise.

"She is. I'm so grateful she's come to see me."

"I don't think you need to be grateful! I'm sure she's really happy to be here. And you're having her friend as well next week, aren't you? That's brilliant! I'd have loved to have had a grandma by the sea!"

"Yes, I suppose I do have my benefits," she'd smiled.

I've noticed a change in Elise lately. She seems a little bit more relaxed. Maybe it's the change in the weather, as all this sunshine can't help but lift your spirits, but I just feel like she's somehow more content these days. It's good to see. She may be old, but she's pretty fit and healthy, and she's certainly got all her marbles, as she laughingly says.

I love the way she talks about being old, and the way people's attitudes towards you change. I'm determined not to make that mistake with her. Or anyone else, for that matter. And it's made me see that maybe age isn't so important. Maybe Ada will enjoy Stevie's company almost as much as Stevie will enjoy hers. There is something there for them both, being only children, and I seem to remember that when I was growing up, I was sometimes glad of an excuse to be childlike again. Perhaps Stevie will provide that opportunity for Ada.

The girls stayed in the sea for quite some time, and when they came out, beads of water glistening on their smooth, young bodies, they were starving.

"Let's go to McGinty's!" said Ada. "Up on the cliffs."

So we piled into my car, and with the windows down we made our happy way up to this lovely café with floor-to-ceiling windows looking almost straight down the cliffs to the rocks and the sea below, water gushing in and out of the pools and crevices. As gulls swooped and glided above the cliff face, and gannets dived head-first into the waters, we had a cream tea for four, which Elise insisted on paying for. Then Ada asked if Stevie wanted to stay over a couple of nights with them, which I hadn't been expecting. The plan had been for me to drop her off at Elise's in the mornings, before work.

"You could stay in Uncle Laurie's old room, couldn't she, Grandma?"

Elise had looked at me. "It's up to you, Maggie. She'd be very welcome to. She can stay all week if she likes! But maybe you'd like her company when you get home from work."

I looked at Stevie. How would she feel about this? I should have known – she was delighted at the prospect.

"All week, though, Elise? Are you sure?" I asked, doubtfully.

"I'm perfectly sure. She'll be company for Ada – God knows I'm not up to surfing, or body boarding, or paddle-boarding, or whatever it is she's got planned for this week. We'll take good care of her. And then you can just get into the office and back when you need to. And your evenings will be free, too…"

There was a little twinkle in her eye as she said that. I know she's aware that Tony will be here this week. It's such an odd thought, that he's going to be working upstairs from me. That our paths might cross from time to time, although luckily it will be Graham who has more to do with him from a work point of view. And I've been wondering if and how I could see him outside of work. I make it more difficult for myself, trying to keep all my little worlds apart. Mum and Julia; Stevie; my work; my friendship with Elise; my relationship with Tony. I'm never in any doubt that the priority is Stevie, and that my life with her is what matters. But I know it can't be everything. God knows, in a handful of years she'll be off, anyway. And that's exactly how it should be. But I don't want to be one of those parents who find themselves suddenly dropped into an echoing, achingly empty life once their child has grown up and gone.

"I tell you what," I said to Stevie. "Let's say a couple of days at first, and see how we go. You're only a few streets away, anyway. I can wave to you on my way past every morning."

"I'll probably be still in bed at that time," Stevie said, looking to Ada for approval.

"Well, OK, I'll wave to Elise, then! Unless you're planning on a few lie-ins as well?"

Elise laughed. "No, that's never been my kind of thing, to be honest. You stay as long as you like, Stevie, as long as your mum's happy with the idea. You know I like a full house, Maggie. All that life around me! I'm happy if you are."

"Well, OK then."

So now I'm all alone, eating my breakfast at the table by the window, where a slice of sunshine is falling across the book I'm reading. I don't have long before I have to leave for work, but now I'm working full-time again, I want to savour these little pockets of time to myself. And tonight, I have a date. So possibly I won't be sitting here on my own this time tomorrow.

# 1994

What seemed strange to Maggie was that, as life went on, and improved in so many ways for their family – Jeff had a promotion, taking Rob's job when he moved on, and consequently they were able to move to a bigger house, and money was less of an obstacle – her parents became more distanced from each other. Their previous closeness, affection and jokiness seemed to have all but disappeared, and relations were at best friendly, at worst strained.

Maybe it was work, she thought. Jeff had longer hours these days, and often had to travel, while Lucy had to take on all of the shipping of the girls to and from dance classes, swimming training, parties and sleepovers, as well as going to work, and looking after Pretzel, their much-loved family dog. At weekends, Jeff was still often working, and their family beach days regularly consisted of just Lucy and the twins, while Jeff stayed at home.

The biggest shock had been when Sarah and Rob had split up. It had been totally unexpected, as far as Maggie could tell. The break-up had occurred sometime when the girls were in their second year at school, and contributed to Rob moving away, and giving up his job, and consequently to Jeff obtaining his promotion, and the Cavendishes moving to a larger house, while Sarah and Stacey had to leave the Old Rectory and moved somewhere smaller, in the same little village that the Cavendishes had moved to. Now, they were on a more even footing, but Maggie felt guilty. She knew they had somehow benefitted from Sarah's and Stacey's misfortune. Although Sarah, to be fair, didn't seem to be doing too badly. She was her usual outgoing, glamorous self, and threw herself into local life, getting involved with the Blooming Beautiful committee and the rural council, which governed local matters like funding for the Blooming Beautiful flowers and plants ("Very convenient," said Lucy) and for the little youth club that the girls attended, for trips to places like the Eden Project.

The girls had all loved the youth club. There were older boys there, which Stacey in particular liked, and it was a good place to hang out. It was the only place to hang out. After all, there was not a lot else to do when you were too old for the park and playground, and too young to drive anywhere, like the beautiful sweeping beaches that were just minutes away by car, but too far to walk to (and too dangerous, along the A-road then the secluded, winding, narrow country lanes).

"What I don't get," said Lucy to Jeff, "is how you and I are both working all the hours God sends, while Sarah isn't working at all, and yet we're living in the same town, in near-identical houses. And her car's nicer than ours."

"Well, that's because Rob's supporting her and Stacey, isn't it? Plus, we've got two of these millstones," said Jeff, ruffling Julia's hair, "while they've only got one."

"Hey! We're not millstones. You're very lucky to have us," said Julia.

"Yes, we're a gift. To be treasured," Maggie added.

"I wouldn't go that far," said their dad.

"I blame Pretzel," said Lucy. "He eats his body weight in food every day."

He was a big dog, for sure. They hadn't known when they'd got him quite how big he was going to be. The farm dog, it seemed, had become very close to the German Shepherd up the road, and consequently, when he was fully grown, Pretzel was a lot bigger than his petite collie mum. He was brave and strong and intelligent, and the whole family loved him. But maybe Maggie loved him most of all. And she was happy to walk him, most of the time. She groomed him, and checked his fur for fleas or ticks, and raced around the garden with him, or kicked the football for him, for hours on end. He never seemed to get tired. But in the evenings, he'd slink upstairs, and jump silently onto her bed, curling himself up as small as he could, knowing that when Lucy found him, she would send him slinking back downstairs again, his tail between his legs.

"Can't he stay up here? Just tonight?" Maggie would wheedle.

"No, you know that it will never be for 'just tonight'. Once that particular floodgate is opened, there will be no stopping it."

"I know." Maggie grinned at her mum, then turned back to her homework.

"You working too hard again, love?" Lucy asked.

"Not *too* hard."

"Well, don't forget to take a break, will you? If only you could send some of your commitment your sister's way."

"I heard that!" Julia shouted through.

"You were meant to!"

Jeff was away in Germany, and the atmosphere in the house was relaxed. Whenever one of their parents was out, or away (more often this was Jeff than Lucy, though she did occasionally escape for a night out with a friend), the other one seemed to unwind a little. Become more lenient. There would be pizza for tea, or fish and chips (cheese and onion pasty in Maggie's case, in place of the fish – she had recently become a committed vegetarian), and late-night hot chocolates. What was it when both parents were there, Maggie wondered, that made them seem to try harder, and be stricter with the girls? It was almost like a competition at times, she thought.

"Hey, Julia," she whispered, when Lucy had gone back downstairs, pulling a reluctant Pretzel with her.

"What?" Julia was listening to music with her headphones on, the cord stretched as far as possible from her midi-system, so that she could just about lie on the bed. It didn't look all that relaxing to Maggie.

"It's Mum and Dad's anniversary next month, isn't it?"

"Er... yeah, I think so."

"Shall we plan something for them?"

"Like what?"

"I don't know. A night away. In a hotel."

"How could we afford that? Anyway, if they're going to stay in a hotel, I want to, too."

"But don't you think they need some time to themselves? Together? Without us?"

Maggie was a keen reader of the weekend magazine that came with the paper, and she read the problem page thoroughly. She knew all about how important it was for couples with children to keep their relationship, and interest in each other, alive.

"What if we ask Stacey if we can stay at hers… and make them a nice meal, maybe get them a bottle of wine to have."

"As if we'd get served!"

"We can ask Sarah to get it for us, dumbo." Maggie was frustrated by her sister's lack of enthusiasm. She had been so sure this was a great idea.

"Go on, then," Julia said, swinging her legs round and sitting up, so that her headphones ended up around her neck.

"Really?"

"Yeah. I guess they deserve something nice."

"They'll love it!" Maggie said. "I just know it."

# Maggie

"You look gorgeous." Tony leans over and kisses me once I'm settled in his passenger seat.

"Well thank you, you don't look so bad yourself." I'm out of breath, and feeling a bit sweaty and nervous, but as he pulls out of the car park and into the road, I take a sneaky look at Tony's profile. He's got a little bit of greying stubble, and a dimple, or perhaps a scar, just above the left corner of his mouth. I had felt slightly on edge all day, knowing he was in the upstairs office today; and I half-expected him to appear at the door at any moment, but I didn't see him at all, though he sent me a couple of messages when I went outside at lunchtime.

**I'm watching you.**

Followed almost immediately by:

**Sorry, that was meant to be funny but actually that sounds really creepy. I was just looking out of the office window and saw you come outside. Looks lovely out there.**

I'd looked up the side of the building, my eyes squinting against the sun, but of course I couldn't see him.

I'll let you off. Aren't you meant to be working, though? Not staring out of the window?

On a conference call. No cameras. They can't see me. I can sit back and listen and admire the view. Sorry. Also creepy. I mean, I am admiring the view across the harbour – although that's not to say I'm not admiring my view of you as well. Oh god I'm terrible at text flirting.

This is you flirting, is it?

Well... trying to. Sorry. Maybe delete those last messages and I'll start again. Pretend this never happened.

Too late! I've got to dash for my lunch anyway.

Have I ruined everything? Is our date tonight still on?

I suppose so.

I had smiled to myself and walked out of sight, back to the house, where I'd left a salad in the fridge. I put on the radio to listen to the news while I ate. I even had time to make sure I had something to wear this evening, picking out a halter-neck top and my favourite Seasalt trousers.

How are you getting on? xxx I messaged Stevie.

Great, Mum! ☺ xxx Her reply was almost instant.

Followed by **Me and Ada are going to the beach this afternoon xxx**

**Wish I was, too! Have a great time. I miss you xxx**

**Love you xxx**

**Love you too xxx**

The afternoon went by very slowly, as I kept checking the clock, and my phone. It's hard letting go of Stevie, and letting somebody else take responsibility for her. Maybe I should have been worried about her going to the beach with somebody I barely know, who, in all honesty, is not much more than a child herself, but I do believe in letting Stevie realise that she can take some responsibility for herself, and I know she's a sensible girl. She knows all about the dangers of the sea – all the kids do, round here. Which is not to say it stops some of them doing crazy stuff like tombstoning, but I know Stevie won't be doing anything like that. I've been worrying it's too much for Elise, too, but I know what she'd have to say if I voiced my concerns to her.

Finally, it was five pm. Graham is very keen that we all finish at five. "There's not much that can't wait," he says, "apart from our families."

I saved the document I was working on, and switched off my computer. The others were doing the same. We left the office together, walking out into the welcoming arms of the afternoon, and went our separate ways – Amy and Graham to their cars, and Sheila up the hill to her house, which is a little out of town, in a little terrace of cottages up near the cliffs. I walked a different way home to normal, for some reason not wanting to pass Elise's. Partly for my benefit, and partly for Stevie's, so she wouldn't think I was checking up on her.

The streets in the summer are dirtier than in the winter. Chip wrappers, picked clean of actual chips by ever-willing gulls; little cardboard lids from Cornettos; cigarette ends, and bottle tops. We do have a street cleaner, going around twice a week. I know in some of the more popular tourist towns, the streets are cleaned every day, bright and early every morning. We could do better here. Maybe that's something I can tie in with work. I made a mental note to look into this, as I reached my front door. Back into my little, empty house, I put on the kettle and ran upstairs for a quick shower and to get changed. I also laid out some clothes for work tomorrow.

I had time for a quick cup of camomile tea, trying to feel calm and relaxed, and then my phone buzzed. Tony.

**I'm ready and waiting.**

Checking doors and windows were closed and locked, I whizzed around the house, then out of the front door, locking it behind me, and through a couple of back streets until I reached the little long-stay car park where we'd agreed to meet. I saw Tony straight away and dashed to his car, checking nobody I knew was nearby.

It seems ridiculous, I know, but I don't want gossip, and

I know full well that gossip is a popular pastime round here. I don't want anyone at work to know I'm seeing one of the bigwigs from Canyon Holdings. And I don't want Stevie to know I am seeing anyone. Not yet. Not until I know that it's somebody worth her knowing about.

We take the road out of town, and I begin to relax. Tony's just taken on the rental of a bungalow that's been built by a local farmer. He's got it on a year's lease, which is nice to know, as it suggests he is here for a while. Though I am sure the company would pick up the tab if they needed him elsewhere.

I'm grateful it is remote, but as he pulls into the driveway, I see just how remote, and a little fear tinges my thoughts. I don't really know Tony, after all. And I've just let him bring me up here to this secluded place, where I apparently have bugger-all phone signal, too.

He sees me looking at the screen. "Ah, yes. You'll need the WiFi password, and you should let Stevie know to WhatsApp you if she needs you." He pulls a card from his wallet with the WiFi details.

"That's all she uses anyway!" I connect to the router, and feel relieved to see I do have some contact with the outside world. I think it is mostly to do with Stevie. With knowing I am her sole parent. I cannot ever allow anything to happen to me, because I am all she has. Of course, it's not quite true. She has Mum, and Julia, and Paul, and friends, but even so…

"Of course. Who'd have thought we'd get to a point when text messages were old school?" He opens his door, and I feel a sharp blast of wind blow in and across me. It's quite exposed up here. I get out of the car, admiring the tidy flowerbeds that border the driveway:

heather and rosemary and lavender gently scenting the air while colourful blooms, on tall, delicate stems, sway and bow slightly in the wind.

"This is lovely," I say, taking a moment to admire it all. I love, really love, being right by the sea, but I can see the appeal of being somewhere like this – with the wide-open skies and the lack of litter, or passers-by. Some way behind his house is a gentle hill, with standing stones, and a scattering of sheep, which bleat intermittently.

"Come on in," Tony says, unlocking the front door. Inside, once the door is closed, it is so quiet. The gentle hum of the fridge and freezer, and the ticking of a clock. The place is neat and tidy, and smells of washing powder. I look around me. Tony's only been in for a couple of days, so has not yet had a chance to really make it his, but I see a couple of photo frames, one with a picture of an older couple, and one of Tony with a teenage boy and girl. "They're my brother's kids," he says. "They're great... and that's my parents. All of them live in Kent. My brother included."

"That's a bit of a drive."

"Yeah, but they're used to me being away. And it's better than when I was in America. Drink?" he asks, holding up a bottle of gin.

"Yes please." I don't want to drink too much, but one would be nice. And it's the perfect day for a gin & tonic. He drops handfuls of ice into two tall glasses, and splashes the gin across it, topping them up with fizzing tonic and a slice of lemon. We take our drinks through to the conservatory.

"This is lovely," I say, sitting on the battered old sofa,

looking out at the garden and across the fields beyond.

"I know. I can't quite believe it. I can't quite believe I like it so much, in fact. It reminds me of home, though. The fields. The farms. The smells. I don't think I'm made for city living anymore."

"I know what you mean." Does this mean Tony might want to stick around? Visions of a future with him flood my mind, though I know it's silly, and I barely know the man. It's hope mixed with fear. What if I fall for him, and he doesn't feel the same about me? Or if he does feel the same, but has to move away? Or if we make a go of it, and he cheats on me? I absolutely cannot risk Stevie being let down like that.

I need to chill out. It's just our second date.

Tony sits on a hard chair, facing me, and we chat about nothing very much. Our days at work. The local area. What it was like for me, growing up by the sea. What it was like for him, going to boarding school. When we've finished our drinks, he asks if I'm hungry, and we go through to the kitchen. I sit at his breakfast bar, sipping my second gin & tonic and shelling and eating pistachio nuts, while he prepares a stir-fry for us both. He's got the radio on, and is humming while he works. I like this. How comfortable it feels. And domestic. Something I have never really experienced before.

I'm a mess when it comes to relationships, I know. Do I trust them? I don't know. I run through my list of examples. Mum and Dad. Well, they loved each other. I know they did. But their marriage wasn't perfect.

Julia and Paul. Now there is a real, solid relationship. A partnership. They are happy together, and trust each other implicitly, in every area of life.

Stacey and Sean. The less said about them, the better.

It's hard to trust, isn't it? And difficult to let somebody in. Not to mention allowing Stevie to become close to somebody, too. I am her everything, and I chose for it to be that way. I could have let her know about her dad – or let her dad know about her, at the very least. But I opted to go it entirely alone. I was justified, or at least I thought I was, at the time, but as the years have moved on, I've come to doubt myself. Is that decision really mine to make?

"Penny for them?" Tony asks, and I think how I haven't heard anyone say that since Dad died.

"Sorry! I was away with the fairies. Just thinking about work," I lie.

"Well, dinner's just about ready, so we can sit and eat, and you can tell me all about it, if you like. Or we can just forget about work, and see where the evening takes us."

He smiles at me – an open, apparently guileless smile, which I can't help but return.

I pick up my glass, and slide off my chair, following him back through to the conservatory, where there is a small table. Tony places the plates down, and pulls back a chair for me. "I thought you'd like to sit here, so you can admire the view."

"Thank you, it's lovely. And the food smells delicious."

"I hope you enjoy it. It's nice to have somebody to cook for."

"It's nice to be cooked for," I smile.

"Good. Cheers," he says, and clinks his glass against mine. "*Bon appetit.*"

# 1994

"What's all this?" Lucy smiled, seeing an envelope on the kitchen table addressed to her and Jeff.

"It's your anniversary, isn't it?" Maggie asked.

"Well, yes, it is. I didn't expect you to remember, though!"

"We wouldn't forget, would we, Julia?"

"No!" Julia looked up from her book. "Well, to be fair, it was Maggie who remembered, really."

Maggie smiled at her sister. Always fair and honest. She loved that about her. "Where's Daddy?" she asked.

"He's just having a shower."

"What have you got him for your anniversary?" Maggie was almost as excited about this day as her birthday. She was determined it would help bring some romance back into Jeff's and Lucy's relationship.

"Oh, erm, nothing. We don't really do that anymore…"

"Nothing?" Maggie was outraged. "It's your wedding anniversary!"

"Yes, but, well, I suppose we've had quite a few of them."

"And that's exactly why you should be celebrating!"

"You're right. Sorry. When did you become such a romantic, anyway? Is there something – or somebody – I should know about?"

"No!" Maggie's face flushed. It was true. While her crush on Robert Bastion had faded, and she'd found other boys to pin her hopes on, none of them had returned her feelings. It was always Stacey and Julia that the boys liked, and more than once Maggie had been approached by somebody, and felt her heartbeat begin to increase in pace and in panic, only to realise that they wanted to know if her sister, or her friend, would go out with them. Maggie would grin, and pretend to take it all in her stride. She'd developed quite a reputation as a tomboy, and the boys seemed to feel comfortable with her, in a way that they weren't with Stacey and Julia. But they never looked at Maggie in a romantic way. It sometimes felt like she would never kiss anybody, or even hold hands with someone. She desperately wanted to know what it felt like. She desperately wanted to feel wanted.

"You're blushing!" Lucy teased, but out of the corner of her eye, Maggie saw Julia look up and shoot a warning look at Lucy, who seemed to catch its meaning immediately. "Well thank you, girls. Shall I wait for Daddy, to open it?"

"Yes! You should definitely open it together."

Soon enough, Jeff came whistling down the stairs, his hair wet, and his golf clothes on.

"You're not playing golf today, Dad?!" Maggie exclaimed.

"I am!" He looked at the three faces before of him. "Aren't I…? Have I missed something?"

"It's your anniversary!"

"Oh, yes, well of course it is," he floundered.

"Had you forgotten?" Julia asked accusingly.

"No! No, of course not."

"Open this, with Mummy," Maggie commanded, pushing the envelope into his hands.

"Thank you, Maggie." Jeff moved next to Lucy, and opened the envelope, pulling out a handmade card, and scattering silver stars all over the table. "What's this?" he asked, smiling.

"Let me see," Lucy said. She opened the card, and took a moment to read it. "Oh. Oh, girls." Her eyes were shining.

Jeff was reading too, a moment behind his wife, and then he looked at her. "That is really thoughtful of you two," he said.

The front of the card was a sketch Maggie had done, from one of her parents' wedding photos. It showed Lucy and Jeff smiling at each other, at the front door to their old house in Bristol. In the photo, the three-year-old twins had been standing beside them, but no matter how hard Maggie had tried, she was not happy with any of her efforts to draw her and her sister's infant forms.

Julia had used her calligraphy set to write the invitation on a sheet of thick cream paper, which was folded and tucked inside the card:

*Lucy and Jeff,*

*You are invited to a celebration of your eleventh wedding anniversary, in the comfort of your own home.*

*Your beautiful daughters will be out for the night, after cooking you an anniversary meal.*

*You never get to go out together and we couldn't*

*afford a hotel so we hope that you will enjoy this just as much.*

*We love you.*

*Julia and Maggie*

"That is really lovely, girls," Lucy said, giving both of her daughters a kiss. "Isn't it, Jeff?"

"It is." Jeff looked like he might cry, Maggie thought.

She flew to his side and hugged him. "You can still go to golf, Dad. As long as you're back in time to get changed for your meal tonight."

"Thank you, Maggie," he smiled. "I'll pick up a bottle of wine on the way back shall I, Lucy?"

"That's all taken care of!" Julia said proudly. "We asked Sarah to get one, with our money."

"Sarah?" Lucy asked.

"Yes! You know... Sarah... your friend... our best friend's mum..."

"We know who Sarah is!" Jeff said, Maggie thought a little sharply. But he quickly recovered himself. "Well, that was nice of her. And did you have enough money for a good bottle?"

"Sarah said so. She picked something to go with your dinner."

"Which is...?"

"You'll have to wait and see!" Maggie danced around the kitchen. "Mum, you can have a bath this afternoon. I'm going to run it for you."

"And I'm going to do your hair and nails," said Julia.

"What about *my* hair and nails?" Jeff teased.

"It's too late for you, Dad! As long as you tell Mum how beautiful she looks."

"I already know she will." Jeff looked at his wife, and she looked away.

"You get off to the golf course, Jeff," Lucy said and turned to her daughters. "It sounds like you girls have got today well planned. But would you fancy a trip to the beach this morning, while Dad's at golf? It's such a beautiful day, I'd love a dip in the sea."

"Yes please, Mum."

"Great. Well, you go and get your beach stuff together, and I might even treat you to lunch out, seeing as you've been so thoughtful."

Maggie and Julia dashed off upstairs together, Pretzel hot on their heels. They went into their bedrooms, shouting to each other as they pulled t-shirts and shorts, towels and swimwear out of their drawers. When they had moved to this new house, they had decided they would be better with their own space each, now they were a little bit older. And their music taste was different. And Julia liked to spend hours on the phone, dragging it into her bedroom and closing the door closed across the over-stretched cord, so that she could have some privacy.

Maggie wanted some solitude, and peace, so that she could work when she needed to, and she had also had enough of Julia moving or losing her things. It had begun to become a bit of a problem between them, and sometimes Maggie felt like Alice, grown too big for the space she was occupying. But now they had their own rooms, and each was responsible for keeping them tidy

– or not. As long as they had their school uniforms organised and neat, and their school books, too, then what they did with the rest of their things was up to them.

"Bye, girls!" shouted Jeff, and they heard the door go.

"Are you two ready?" Lucy called.

"Yes! Can we bring Pretzel?"

"Of course!"

"Yay! Did you hear that, Pretzel? We're going swimming!" Maggie laughed as he jumped up and licked her face. He was easily as tall as she was when he was on his hind legs.

The four of them piled into Lucy's car, Pretzel turning round a few times to settle himself in the boot. Julia was in the front alongside Lucy, and Maggie on the back seat, so she could reach her arm back and stroke the dog.

Arriving at the car park, they could see there were already a few people in the sea, and plenty of little groups setting up for the day, which promised to be hot and sunny. Any other weekend and Maggie would have been pushing for a whole day at the beach herself – she loved nothing more than staying well into the evening, when most of the other beach-goers had left for home, and they could have the sand and the waves almost to themselves – but today she was keen to get home as well. She and Julia had been consulting the cookbooks in the house, and come up with a menu for their parents: bruschetta with mozzarella, tomato and basil to start; vegetable lasagne with garlic bread and salad for mains; lemon cheesecake for dessert. Maggie was in charge of the lasagne and salad, while Julia was doing the bruschetta and cheesecake.

"You have to stay clear of the kitchen this afternoon, Mum," Julia said. "If you want a cup of tea, you're going to have to ask us for it."

"Well, I think I could just about cope with that!" Lucy smiled. "Maybe I'll have an hour or two reading in the garden. Today just gets better and better!"

"What time will Dad be back?"

"I'm not sure. He's usually back mid-afternoon, isn't he?"

"And we're going to Stacey's at five. You'll have to put the la… something in the oven, but it will be all ready for you. Just don't forget, will you?" Maggie asked anxiously.

"No, I won't forget! I promise. This is really lovely of you two, you know."

"We know!" Julia grinned.

"Modest, aren't you?"

"Yep."


They found a spot near the rocks at the back of the beach, to leave their towels and bags, and then they raced down to the shore, Pretzel dancing around them, barking with over-excitement.

"Last one in's a rotten egg!" Lucy shouted, mimicking the Enid Blyton books that the girls once used to love.

"Ha ha, Mum!" Julia looked around to make sure there was nobody around to have heard what Lucy said. She was definitely developing a sensitivity towards her street cred.

The beach shelved sharply at this point and, with the tide in, it was easy to be fully immersed in seconds.

Maggie took the opportunity to plunge on in, leaving Julia slightly behind her.

"Looks like you're the rotten egg, Julia!" she laughed.

"I think that's Pretzel, actually." Their dog stayed on the shoreline, barking at them, and retreating from the frothing incoming waves.

"Come on, Pretzel! Come on, boy!" He always took some persuading. Lucy, Maggie and Julia all called him, but in the end Maggie had to go and physically coax him across the shallows, then throw a couple of stones into the water so that he chased them in, and before he knew it, though he had no chance of finding those stones, he was swimming, and remembering that he really enjoyed it.

They never went too far or too deep when Pretzel was with them, but he swam between the three of them, and showed no signs of tiring, until after a while Julia and Maggie decided to head back in to shore, and sit drying out in the sun.

Lucy stayed in the water for a little while longer, and the girls watched her ploughing back and forth, parallel to the beach, just far enough out that she was unhindered by the other swimmers, or families with dinghies and body boards.

"You're a pretty good swimmer for an old lady," Maggie ventured when Lucy returned, the beads of saltwater sparkling on her skin.

"Watch it, young lady!" Lucy grinned, and shook her hair over her daughter, causing Pretzel to leap up and bark.

They lay on their towels, each lost in their own thoughts for a while. Maggie was running through what she and Julia needed to do that afternoon. She hoped Julia was, too, but had a feeling that her sister's mind might actually be preoccupied with Matthew Wilson, a fourth year at school. Maggie hoped very much that Lucy was looking forward to her evening. As for Pretzel… well, who knew what he thought about? He lay next to her, his body stretched alongside hers, and Maggie curled her arm around him, burying her face in his damp fur. He smelled of the sea. She listened to the familiar sounds of the beach: children shouting and laughing; the waves rolling in, then pulling back out again; seagulls shrieking high above. She would like to record it, she thought, and play it to herself when she was going to sleep.

The sea swim had made them hungry, and they decided they needed chips, so they stuffed their towels back into the bags, and pulled clothes back on over now-dry swimwear. With sand stuck to their skin and burrowed deep into their hair, the four of them happily made their way back to the car, and headed along the coast to a fish & chips van that they knew would be in its usual place, at a layby with a far-reaching view of the sea. Scattering salt and vinegar liberally over their chips, they headed for a free bench, Pretzel staying obediently at their sides, his attention focused solely on those hot, paper-wrapped packages. Lucy had bought three cans of Dandelion and Burdock, and opened each in turn.

"We are old enough to open our own cans you know, Mum," Julia reminded her.

"I do know. Of course, I know. But humour me. I need to be needed, you know."

"We still need you," Maggie said. "Who else would drive us to our friends' houses?"

"Or take me to dance?" Julia asked.

"OK, I see, and soon it'll be parties, and then it'll be college, then uni, then you'll be gone." Lucy's gaze stretched far out across the waves.

"We'll still need you then, Mum," Maggie said, knocking gently into her arm.

"We'll always need you," said Julia, from their mum's other side.

Lucy put an arm around each of her daughters. "I love you more than you can ever know."

Pretzel put his head on Maggie's leg, and dribbled a little. He had no time for such sentimentality. Not when there were chips to be had.

# Maggie

At the weekend, Mum arrives. Before she heads to the flat where she'll be spending the next month or so, she stops at our place, to be greeted by a very, very excited Stevie.

"Grandma!" she says, throwing herself into Mum's arms, while I stand just behind her. I must admit I am excited to see her, too. This is the first time Mum's been to our house, and I hope she likes it. It's so small compared to back home, and I know she might wonder why I have swapped that for this, but I spent all last night tidying, cleaning, hoovering, and even polishing, to make the house look the best it can be. It's not like I think Mum would judge me if it was a bit of a mess, but I want her to see how well we're managing. But then I worry, will it hurt her feelings that Stevie and I are managing so well without her?

"Well, this place is lovely!" she says, looking around her, then coming to me and hugging me tight. "It reminds me a bit of the house in Bristol!"

"It's not very big," I say.

"Well, no, but it doesn't have to be, does it? And what a lovely town, too. Is that where you work, that big, glossy building by the harbour? It looks very impressive."

"It is. It's not exactly popular with the locals, though."

"Ah well, it may be more popular than you think. It's always the dissenting voices that are heard loudest."

My mind flicks to the local Facebook group. "That is very true."

"Maybe some people will love it. Especially if they've got young children, or are youngsters themselves, looking for work. Anyway, you can show me around the place in good time! I'm gasping for a cup of tea right now."

"Well, we can soon fix that, can't we, Stevie? Do you want to make your grandma a cuppa?"

"Sure. Do you have milk and sugar, Grandma?"

I could answer that question. I know Mum's answer so well: "No sugar, a splash of milk, please."

Stevie scoots off.

"Come in, Mum. Come and have a seat."

"She's growing up," Mum murmurs.

I look at her to see if she's sad to be missing out, but she's just smiling fondly. She follows me into the lounge, gently exclaiming at the pictures on the walls, and the throws and cushions, which Stevie and I chose together. We had to start from scratch, really, when we moved down here. I had my own place once, and my own furniture, but I sold it all before I moved back in with Mum. So it was a nice project for me and Stevie, to visit the second-hand and charity shops, scour the local papers, websites and Facebook groups, to try and source what we needed. I did buy us new mattresses, and bedding, but other than that, most things we have are 'pre-loved'.

I realise I've been nervous about having her here, but I should have known there was no need. If I'm happy, and Stevie is, then Mum will be, too. It's funny, though, how whenever I see her, it makes me miss her more.

"How are you, Mum?" I ask now. We can hear the kettle boiling in the kitchen, and Stevie pottering about. I know she's putting out some biscuits she's baked, to surprise Mum with.

"I'm very well, Maggie. Pretty much the same as ever! Although, I have to tell you, I'm thinking of retiring soon."

"Really?"

"Yes. I think it's about time, really. I've started to realise I'm getting bored. Maybe a little boring, too! I don't want that to happen to me. I just… I don't know… I feel like a change." Her eyes are on the street outside, as a couple wander by hand-in-hand. I wonder what she thinks of this narrow network of roads, where my view is of the house opposite, and cars pass by really quite close to the front window. It's a far cry from the tall hedges and beautiful gardens surrounding her house.

"I think you might have sparked it, Maggie. Coming down here, I mean. It was lovely, having you and Stevie living with me. But I could see why you'd want to start again, somewhere new." She doesn't know the half of it, I think. "And I'm not saying I want to do that, exactly, but I do want to shake life up a bit. Try some new things. Meet some new people."

Does she mean men? Or a man? I wouldn't blame her. She was a relatively young widow, and she's only in her sixties now. Why shouldn't she want to meet somebody? Have a companion? Or fall madly in love. Although the thought of that makes me ache for Dad. I do sometimes feel that for him, like he is missing out, while we've all moved on – or carried on, at least. He never got to meet Stevie. He never saw Julia's dance school. Never got to come on any more days out with us, or holidays, or anything. Everything just stopped, for him. And sometimes, if I catch myself feeling happy, I squash it. I make myself think of him, and what happened, and that I shouldn't really be happy. That it isn't fair.

But Mum, and Dad, would tell me to be happy. To be as happy as I can, and that life isn't guaranteed, and nor is happiness, which makes it all the more precious. If I could just learn to relax, I think I could do it. But there is too much going on in my head.

"That sounds really good, Mum. If you're sure you won't miss work too much."

"I don't think so! I've done my time." She laughs. "Anyway, I haven't made any real plans yet. I'm just thinking about it. I'll keep you informed. And I might want to bounce some ideas off you, as well!"

"Any time, Mum."

Stevie appears with a tray, with three cups of tea, and a plate of shortcake.

Mum takes her cup gratefully, and one of the biscuits. It is a bit misshapen, and clearly homemade, but Mum says, "These look nice. Where did you buy them from?"

"I made them!" Stevie exclaims, looking fit to burst with pride.

"You never did!"

"I did. Mum helped a bit, didn't you, Mum?"

"Yes, but Stevie found the recipe online, and worked it all out herself. I just had to help a bit with making sure the butter was soft enough, and with the oven."

Mum takes a bite, sugary crumbs falling from her mouth. "Well, this is delicious. And you are very clever, Stevie." She puts her arm out, and Stevie sinks down into the seat next to her. They look very çosy. It makes me happy and sad at the same time.

"When are we going to your house, Grandma?"

"It's not quite my house!" she laughs. "But we can go whenever you like, Stevie."

"Shall we go after this?" I ask. I'm keen to go and see the place, too. Mum's friend Seren is an artist, and apparently her home is a penthouse apartment, with an art studio that has huge windows to look out across the roofs of the town, and a roof terrace. It sounds right up my street, but I am very unlikely to ever be able to afford a place like that.

"Yes! I'm glad you said that! I'm really excited to see it. In fact, I can't wait! I've bought myself an easel, and some watercolours, and I'm going to give it a go while I'm here. I thought you might like to as well, Stevie. And you, Maggie?" she suggests. "If you've got time?"

I feel like she is being cautious in her approach to me, like she doesn't want to encroach on my new life.

"I would love that, Mum. Honestly, I am so happy you're here. I want to spend as much time with you as I can. And a bit of painting sounds brilliant!"

I'm touched at how pleased Mum looks, but I can understand it. It won't be long before Stevie has her own life, and won't want to spend anywhere near as much time with me. I hope that when she's my age, we'll still do things together.

We chat easily over our tea and biscuits, and Stevie gives Mum a tour of the house, which doesn't take long.

Then we all pile into Mum's car, and head out of town and along past the estuary, windows down, and the wind in our hair.

# 1994

In the afternoon, the girls shut Lucy out of the kitchen, Julia making a sign which read 'Parents Keep Out', and sticking it to the glass of the door with Blu Tack.

The twins busied themselves finding the ingredients they needed, and giving in occasionally to ask Lucy where something was. Maggie got out her school home economics book and found the recipe for the lasagne, while Julia looked through the bookshelf for the cheesecake recipe.

They turned Radio One on and sang along to the songs they knew as they worked, talking and laughing with each other.

"Are you two OK in there?" Lucy would ask sporadically.

"Yeah!"

"Keep out!"

"OK, OK," she'd laugh. "I get the message. I do feel kind of redundant, though."

"Mum, you're always saying you want a break. So take it."

"Fine! You're right. But can I just sneak in for…"

"No!" the girls shouted together.

"Just tell us what you want, and we'll get it," Maggie said.

"Yes, stop being such a control freak, Mum!"

Lucy laughed and gave in.

Maggie almost didn't want the afternoon to end. It was so nice just being with her sister. They spent so much time with Stacey, who did somehow seem to find her way to being centre of attention, whatever they were doing. In the kitchen that afternoon, it felt like the girls had rediscovered the balance between themselves, and, when the food was made, and they were clearing and washing up, Maggie was pleased when Julia said, "This has been so nice. You're not bad for a twin."

"You're alright too, I suppose," Maggie grinned.

"We'd better get ready to go, though. Dad'll be back soon."

"I guess."

They closed the door behind them and went upstairs.

"Want to get changed in my room?" Julia asked. "We can put one of your records on if you like."

"Yeah! That would be great."

"We're just getting changed," Julia called through to Lucy, who was sitting in the lounge, watching *Murder, She Wrote*, Pretzel spread out across her lap.

"I don't think I could move if I wanted to!" Lucy laughed.

"You'd better get changed for dinner, though, Mum," Julia said. "That nice green dress."

"Oh, really? Do I have to? It's not like we're going out…"

Maggie knew what she meant, but they were determined that tonight would be romantic for their parents. "Sorry, Mum, but this is like a date for you and Dad. You need to look nice. We're going to make Dad wear a suit."

"In this heat?"

"Well, a shirt and trousers, at least."

"Alright, seeing as you've made such an effort."

The twins grinned at each other. While they got

changed and Julia somehow talked Maggie into letting her put some make-up on her, they heard the front door, and Pretzel barking, then Lucy and Jeff laughing.

"Stay out of the kitchen, Dad!" Julia opened her door a crack to shout the order. "And your suit's out in the bedroom."

"Yes, sir!" Jeff called up. They could hear the smile in his voice.

The house felt full of happiness.

Lucy took the twins over to Stacey's. "I'll just drop you at the end of the drive," she said. She'd been doing this for a while; now the girls were older, she no longer seemed to feel any need to go and see Sarah. Maggie hoped Sarah didn't mind. She felt sorry for her since Rob had left, and thought she must be lonely. She'd have expected her mum to make more of an effort to include Sarah in things, as that was Lucy's way, but she could see the two women were very different.

"You need to come and get the bottle of wine, Mum," Julia said.

"Yes, Sarah said she'd keep it chilled. It's the sparkling one you like."

"Oh, girls!" Lucy said. "I'd forgotten all about that! Can one of you run it back down the drive for me? I can't really leave the car here."

"You could just pull in, Mum."

"Oh, but I'm facing the wrong way now. I'd have to go down the road and come back again. Go on, it won't take you a minute."

So Maggie fetched the wine – "Thank you, Sarah!" – running back to her mum's car, where Lucy was fiddling with the radio. "Here you go, Mum."

"That is so lovely of you. Thank you, Maggie. Please say thanks to Sarah, too. And hi to Stacey."

"You could have come and said it yourself."

"Maybe next time."

"Alright! Well, get home now, and drive safely. You look lovely. I hope you like your food. We left all the instructions with it all in the fridge."

"You are absolutely brilliant. Thank you so much, and Julia. I'm so proud of you both." With a tear or two in her eyes, Lucy drove away, and Maggie stayed for just a moment, surprised at the sudden feeling of not wanting her mum to go, or perhaps of wanting to be in the car with her. It was like there was a length of invisible elastic, pulling taut with the distance between them. She felt almost a panic, at the thought it might stretch and snap, and something might happen to Lucy. It was irrational, and babyish. She needed to grow up. With a long, determined inhale, she turned on her heel, and walked back towards the house, where her sister and their friend, and a large cheese and tomato pizza, awaited her.

# Maggie

I think I love my job! It's just so good, to feel like I've really got something to get my teeth into again, after all this time. Don't get me wrong. I love being a mum – most of the time. I think, going by what other mums have said, I've been pretty lucky with Stevie so far. But we have yet to hit the teenage years. Maybe she's been saving it all up for then.

This is something different, though. The time to be myself – even though I'm working. And being trusted to get on with my work, and come up with ideas, which Graham actually listens to. It's giving me a huge boost, and I feel like my confidence is growing every day. I like being an adult amongst other adults.

Now, my contract is only for two years, because that is as long as the Saltings Social Enterprise has funding for. It will be down to us to secure more funding for a longer term, if we can. But right now, we are just getting started. We have Monday morning team meetings, where we discuss our plans for the week. Sheila and Amy are invited to contribute their ideas, and use their local knowledge, for projects and schemes. Graham and I are making contact with local groups, to see how we might work with them. There is so much going on here in this small town.

So far, the response has been more or less positive,

despite some grumblings about the Saltings development. Most of these groups are self-funded, and always looking for ways to raise cash. We have some money we can offer as grants, but these must be applied for, and we can also offer practical help, in terms of providing a space for people to meet, and resources for activities. Honestly, I love it. There is so much we can do, and when people start to see that this place can have a positive impact, it will be a win-win for all of us.

My mind flicks often to some of the oldies, though, who will be perhaps the hardest to win over. Bill, Sylvia, Eleanor, Jack. All people I chatted with and played cards with at the club. I haven't seen them since, and I feel like I can imagine the way they think of me now I've joined the dark side.

"But some people will never accept change, Maggie," Graham says, when I voice this concern to him. "And think about it – this is the only home they've ever known. They've already seen it go from a functional fishing town to a semi-tourist attraction. Not as bad as some of the places further along the coast, I grant you. But it's not what they used to know. And it is annoying, having strangers walking past your front room window, and eyeing up your place for a second home. Hoping you pop your clogs soon, so they can snap up a bargain."

I laugh. "I know, it must feel like that! And I do get it. I really do. I feel torn, sometimes. I remember when I moved here, and heard all about the Saltings, I was determined to hate it as well. Am I a hypocrite now, working here?"

"No, you're not. No more than I am, anyway. I'm no big fan of companies like Canyon, but sometimes you've got to work alongside them, or even inside them, to make sure your voice is heard. Add a bit of balance."

"I guess you're right. I'm sure you are. I still feel like I need to avoid all the old folk, though," Except for Elise, I think. She's a bit more open to all this. She's one in a million, that woman.


I drop in to see her after work, as I'm aware that since she had Stevie to stay, I've not seen her. And Ada and her friend will have gone back to London by now.

"I hope I'm not interrupting anything," I say, when she opens the door.

"Well, I was just on the phone to the United Nations, but I'll call them back," she smiles, and I laugh. "Come in, Maggie. It's lovely to see you. How's the new job?"

"Oh, it's... well, to be honest, Elise, it's great. Does that make me a traitor to the town?"

"Of course not! We've already been through all this. You're perfectly entitled to work wherever you please."

"Is my name mud, at Caring the Community?"

"No! No, not at all. You can put that thought right out of your head. Anyway, those old buggers love having something to complain about. Imagine if they took the Saltings away now... they'd be devastated."

She puts the kettle on, and I sit at the little table. "Did you have a good time with Ada?"

"Oh yes, it was lovely to have her here. And Stevie, too. It fair flew by, though."

"I know, it must feel a bit quiet now."

"It does that. I like my own space, as you know, but I wouldn't mind a few more visitors. I suppose Stevie's with your mum now?"

"She is, she's staying with her this week."

"Well, that's nice, for the two of them. It'll be good for you and your mum to spend some time together."

Of course, Elise thinks that things between Mum and me have been less than rosy. How can I have let her think that? I feel guilty towards her, and towards Mum.

"Cup of tea?" Elise asks.

"Yes please, Elise. And yes, it is really good, having Mum here. I think Stevie's pleased to see her, too."

"I'm sure. And how is your sister getting on, without your mum back home?"

"She's... fine, thanks, Elise." I am momentarily puzzled by the question, but, of course, I misled her there too, didn't I? OK, let's be honest (for once) – I outright lied to her. She thinks Julia's got three sons, doesn't she? And that she's one of those women who relies on their mum to still do everything for them. I feel my cheeks flush. I hope Elise doesn't notice.

"Good, good." She busies herself pouring the boiling water into the mugs.

"How is your daughter? Louisa?" I ask, as though I need to remind her of her daughter's name. "Is she still planning to visit?"

"Yes, I think so! I hope so! Unless work calls. But I think she's determined to get here this summer. Says she needs a break. Between you and me, I think she's starting to change a bit in her attitude towards her job. Maybe she's gone as far as she wanted to, and she's certainly proven herself, more than once. She's no spring chicken either, of course. I sometimes wonder if that's why her chap finished things. He was younger than her."

"Well, that's a bit superficial of him, if that's the reason they broke up. I'm sure he's not worthy of her, if that's the case."

"No, no, happen you're right. I'd have liked to have met him, though. Found out what it is Louisa looks for in a man. I've honestly no idea. And how is your new beau, anyway?"

She knows that will make me laugh. We talked once about the things people used to say about relationships: courting, and walking out, and going steady. I said I liked the romance of those older times, but she told me not to be fooled, and that it wasn't all flowers and dances, and I felt stupid, remembering that she'd had a bad time in her marriage.

"My new *suitor*," I say, making her smile, "is very well, thank you."

Tony is in London tonight, but will be back tomorrow. We've already arranged to see each other, and I have to stifle my guilt at the thought of Stevie and Mum just a handful of miles away. But I'll be with them on Friday. I'm staying over there for the weekend. I'm looking forward to it. It will be like a holiday, even though it's literally seventeen minutes' drive away.

"I'm glad to hear it. And he's settling in to life in Cornwall, is he?"

"I think so. He seems to like it."

"He'll not be the first Londoner to get a taste for the Cornish life."

I sometimes forget Elise was from London originally. Her school was evacuated here, to Tregynon Manor, in the Second World War, and she never went back. Her mum died, and she stayed on here, with one of her old teachers, until she got married. She hasn't really told me all that much about that time, but I know it wasn't happy. Her husband died young, though, and Elise brought up her two children here, in this very house. The idea of such longevity appeals to me.

While Elise goes to use the bathroom, I sit in the quiet comfort of her home. She has the advantage of being on one of the roads right on the edge of the town. There are no houses opposite her; just the pavement and road, and then it's just a short walk down to the beach. I know she's had offers on this place, but she has resisted, and I doubt very much that any amount of money would convince her to sell up.

When she returns, I tell her a bit about the plans we are making at work, and she listens eagerly. "It sounds wonderful," she says. "Really. You'll soon have the likes of Bill eating out of your hand. And you're a shining example to your girl, you know. It's good for her to see you going to work. I remember my mum in her nurse's uniform. I used to think I'd be a nurse, too, but times change."

She looks sad, and goes quiet for a while. I wonder what she's thinking, and I imagine being able to peer inside somebody else's head. To examine their thoughts, their hopes, their dreams. Is everyone full of self-doubt, and anxiety, and a jumble of thoughts and worries and fears? Or is it just me?

What would somebody see if they could look inside my mind? I imagine a ball of wool which has become tangled. The harder I tug at it, the tighter the knots become. It's been so long since I knew what it was like to really relax – to believe that I am entitled to. Over the years, I've allowed my shoulders to hunch forwards, as though they're carrying the weight of the world. But things are starting to change. I'm beginning to feel happy. Which is wonderful, but also a little bit terrifying.

# 1994

It seemed like the anniversary meal had done the trick. When Sarah dropped the girls off on Sunday – she, like Lucy, no longer bothered to come in and say hello – the house was quiet. They heard the scramble of Pretzel getting out of his bed, his nails clicking on the hard wooden floor of the downstairs as he came to greet them, but their parents were nowhere to be seen.

"Sshh!" Julia put her finger to her lips after she had greeted Pretzel. While Maggie hugged their dog to her, Julia crept up the stairs, then back down again.

"They're still in bed!" she whispered. She and Maggie pulled faces at each other, but also couldn't help grinning.

"I'll let Pretzel out," said Maggie. She took him to the back door, as quietly as she could, but she heard her mum's voice.

"Girls! Is that you?"

"Yes! Who else?" Julia laughed. "You're never still in bed at this time? You're wasting your life away!"

"Yes, you've missed the best part of the day!" Maggie said, and the girls laughed at their role-reversal.

"I heard that!" Jeff – the usual source of such remarks – called downstairs. "We're getting up now, don't worry."

"And thank you, again, girls. That dinner was so nice," said Lucy, appearing at the banister, pulling a cardigan on over her pyjamas.

"And the wine!" Jeff said, appearing at his wife's side. Lucy looked at him and smiled, and he put his arm around her. He was wearing his jogging bottoms, his top half bare.

"Put some clothes on, you two. It's the middle of the day!" Maggie said, laughingly.

"Fine," Jeff pretend-huffed. He and Lucy disappeared back into their room while the twins inspected the kitchen.

"Looks like they ate it all!" Maggie said.

"And they've cleaned up after themselves."

"Good."

Jeff appeared at the doorway. "Your mum's just having a shower. Are you checking up on us?"

"Yes, well, we didn't want you leaving the place a mess."

"As if! And it was lovely, girls, thank you. Honestly, delicious."

"And you had a nice evening?"

"We did. We sat in the garden, until it was dark. It was really relaxing. And so… quiet!" He grinned.

"I expect you missed us, though," said Julia.

"Oh yes, of course."

"I should think so, too."

"Your mum and I thought we could go for a walk this afternoon, the four of us."

"To the beach?"

"We thought maybe along by the river, actually. Somewhere a bit different – with a bit more shade. Where Pretzel can stretch his legs, too. You up for it?"

Maggie was tired, and had homework to do, but she could do it later. It was so long since they'd done anything as a family, she realised. She didn't want to be the one to break this up. "Sounds great, Dad," she said. "Doesn't it, Julia?"

"Sure," said her sister, and smiled.

When Lucy came downstairs, they made sandwiches

and bottles of cold drinks, got sunscreen and sun hats, and sturdy walking shoes, then called Pretzel, and the five of them got in the car, heading out into the heat of the afternoon.

It proved to be the perfect walk. Just over three miles, most of which followed the valley by the river, along a dusty path and crossing the water by means of an old stone bridge, before walking back the other way to the car. They passed the odd fisherman sitting quiet as a mouse, and occasionally other walkers, but by and large it was just them – and Pretzel, who dashed between the four of them, as happy as any of them to be part of a complete family unit. Jeff and Lucy even held hands, Maggie noticed, and she nudged Julia, who smiled and nodded.

In full leaf, the abundant trees provided plenty of shade, and high above buzzards called to each other, revelling in the still, cloud-free day.

Where the river widened and the bank sloped gently down into the sun-dappled water, they stopped and took off their shoes for a paddle, throwing stones for Pretzel to chase. Tiny minnows and bullheads darted away from them.

They sat on the bank and ate their sandwiches, letting their feet dry in the sun, then headed back towards the car.

"It seems a shame to just go straight home," said Lucy, when they were all in the car, windows open to let out some of the trapped heat.

"Pub?" suggested Jeff.

"Yes!" they all shouted.

In the garden of the King's Arms, they sat at a table, Pretzel more than happy to lie in the shade and take big, greedy laps of water from a large tin bowl. The girls had crisps and glasses of apple juice, while Jeff had a pint of bitter and Lucy opted for a pint of shandy.

"This is the life," Jeff said, looking around his family and feeling like he hadn't really seen them for quite some time. Not noticed them, not properly. The girls were so grown-up, and looking less like each other than they used to, but they seemed closer today, he thought, than they had for a while.

And there was Lucy. His wife. Looking tanned and lovely, and happier than she had for ages. Which was his fault, he knew.

"Why are you looking at us like that, Daddy?" Maggie asked.

Ah, Maggie. Always a little bit sharper than Julia. Always checking out what was going on.

"Just you lot, Mags," he smiled at her. "My family. I love you all, you know."

Lucy looked away at first, but then she met his eye. "You soft bugger," she said, but gently, and he knew she meant it as anything but an insult. He felt tears threatening, and was grateful that Pretzel chose that moment to jump up at him. "Yes, OK mate," he laughed. "You, too. I wouldn't leave you out, would I?" The dog licked his face, saving him any further embarrassment.

That evening, Maggie worked late to finish her homework. She didn't mind. It was light until gone 10pm anyway, and she could hear the birds singing in the garden. When the blackbirds began their goodnight calls, she closed her exercise book, and slipped it into her school bag. This had been a good day. A great day. A great weekend, in fact. She felt suddenly very sorry for Stacey, who didn't have what she and Julia did. A real, indisputable, family unit, all safe and sound, and happy together.

# Maggie

It's an unseasonably windy day today, and it is set to get worse. The Met Office has issued warnings that the storm heading our way will affect the West Country, from the Isles of Scilly up to Somerset, and we've been told not to travel unless absolutely necessary. I'd had plans to go over to see Mum and Stevie tonight. I'm missing Stevie so much, and I really want to spend time with Mum while she's here. Graham's suggested I take a couple of days' leave so I can see her, but I don't know. It seems a bit soon for that. And I don't want to be the first one in the office taking days off.

"Shall we do it tomorrow instead?" I had called Mum this morning, before I left for work.

"I think that might be for the best. Don't worry, we've got plenty to occupy ourselves here, haven't we, Stevie?" I heard my daughter's voice in the background. "I must admit I'm quite looking forward to watching the stormy sea from up here. We'll do some baking, and maybe some painting, and watch a film or two. We'll be grand. And we'll look forward to seeing you tomorrow, love. You just make sure you don't get blown away yourself, OK?"

"I'll try not to!" I laugh, but I can't help feeling a bit left out. It should be me doing those things with Stevie. Or with Mum. In fact, embarrassingly, when I hang up

I realise I'm a bit teary.

Now I'm at my desk, looking out over the harbour, which is sheltered, but still not immune to the effects of the brewing storm. The sky is grey and angry, and the water in the harbour is restless. The fishing boats are safely secured, and confidently bob over the waves that rock them. They've seen it all before. Litter blows around in miniature tornadoes, and I see somebody's umbrella skid across the ground, and over the chains by the harbour, into the water, before the poor woman can catch up with it.

As the day goes on, the storm grows in strength, and the noise it makes against our building is distracting. The wind whistles and rails against the windows, but it can't get in. It's hard to hold a phone conversation, though, and so I spend much of the day drafting documents and proposals, and answering the emails that have stacked up.

I message Stevie from time to time:

**How's the storm where you are? xxx**

**It's wild! Amazing! We're trying to paint it xxx**

**What a great idea. I can't wait to see it. I miss you xxx**

**I miss you too. We're making chocolate cake later. xxx**

**Well make sure you save some for me to have tomorrow, OK? xxx**

**OK. Well, I'll try to.xxx**

I picture that little smile of hers, that will be on her face when she types this last message. My stomach contracts at the thought of her, I miss her so much. My phone buzzes again. It's Tony.

**You alright down on the first floor?**

**Yes. It's a bit noisy, though. How's life in the upper echelons?**

**It's really noisy! And a bit scary. Don't tell anyone. Are you busy later?**

**No. Well, I was. I was meant to be seeing Mum and Stevie but we're delaying till tomorrow.**

**Fancy sitting out the storm together?**

**That sounds good.** I take a deep breath. **Why don't you come to me? It's literally four minutes' walk from here and maybe better than driving out of town if this storm really does get worse.**

**I'd love to.**

This is a step forward for me, and I hope I don't regret it. Although Tony did stay over at mine before, it wasn't really planned – and he was out again sharpish in the morning. Now, I'm inviting into my home, and it feels like a big deal to me. Maybe to some people it would be nothing. And it's not like Stevie will be there. But it feels momentous, somehow. And once it's done, I start to think about what I should cook him, and what we'll have to drink, and whether the house is tidy…

**I'll have to pop round to see my friend on the way back from work, make sure she's OK and doesn't need anything. What if you come round a bit after six?**

**Perfect X**

I could just phone Elise, but I know full well she'd say she's fine and in need of nothing. If I drop by, I can just call in and see if she's got enough bread, milk, etc. I know the storm shouldn't last more than the night, but it can't be very nice if you feel you can't go out. I mean, Elise is pretty fit for her age, but she definitely won't want to brave this weather. And she shouldn't.

When I leave the building at the end of the day, it's a struggle between me and the wind to keep the door open long enough to get out. My hair is whipped up into the air immediately, and I'm very glad I am wearing trousers, not a skirt. I hurry along away from the harbourside, and into the relative safety of the streets, down a back alleyway adjacent to Elise's terrace, then round to her front door.

"Maggie!" she says, ushering me in. "What are you doing here? You should be going straight home in this weather. Not that you're not very welcome, of course."

The door shutting behind us is a relief. With no houses opposite, Elise's house is on the front line against the elements.

"Well, it's just a flying visit, I'm afraid. I'm on the way to the shop to pick up some things for dinner, and wondered if you needed anything."

"Oh, you shouldn't have bothered! No, I've got everything I need. But thank you. And if it's dinner, not tea, do I gather you've got somebody joining you?"

I blush. "Yes, erm, Tony's coming round."

"How wonderful! You shouldn't be wasting your time here, though. Go on, get on your way. But thank you, for thinking of me."

"Well, just let me know if you realise you do need anything, OK?"

"I'll be just fine. I love storm-watching. And anyway, I've got some preparation to do, because Louisa's coming next week. And Ada, too!"

"Oh, that's good news, Elise. I bet you can't wait."

"I can't."

"I'll try and see you before then, but if I don't, let's go out one day on the bank holiday weekend, shall we?"

"That sounds lovely. Now go on, shoo!"

I laugh, and pull my jacket around me as I head back out into the wild. On to the general store, where I pick up some salad and crusty bread, and a block of halloumi. I ask for a bottle of red wine, and a bottle of white, and at the last minute I pick up a large bar of dark chocolate as well.

"You take care out there, Maggie," says Gerald, the shopkeeper, and I feel incredibly touched that he knows my name. This little town is really beginning to feel like home.

Through the narrow streets, I am worried about loose tiles skidding off rooftops and clunking me on the head.

It would be incredibly bad luck, but not out of the question. It's a relief to be home, and I hurriedly dump my bags in the kitchen, putting the white wine in the fridge, and run upstairs for a shower. It's a welcome relief as the hot water pours down and the steam envelops me. I could stay here for ages, but I have things to do, and I really should have some clothes on when Tony gets here.

I opt for jeans, a long-sleeved top, and a cardigan – blow-drying my hair and clipping it up messily. I close Stevie's bedroom door. I feel bad I've got a guest here that she knows nothing about, and besides, she deserves her privacy. It's been weird, going to bed without her in the next room. Usually, the last thing I do before I go to bed myself is go in and kiss her goodnight while she's sleeping. She might murmur, and reach for my hand, and I will sit on her bed for a minute or two, before easing my fingers out from her grasp and slipping away to my own room.

Back down the stairs and into the kitchen. I consider pouring myself a glass of wine, but will that make me look like an alcoholic, if I'm already drinking before he gets here? While I'm chopping the halloumi, there is a knock on the door, and I rush to open it. By the sound of things, the storm's really taking control out there.

"Hello! Can I come in?" Tony says, brandishing two bottles of wine. Red and white. The very same brands I'd bought.

"Of course!" I step back to allow him entry. This is not a big house, and there is not a lot of room to manoeuvre in this hallway. He closes the door behind him, and almost shyly offers me the wine.

"You won't believe it, but I've just bought these very same ones," I say, now feeling a little bit shy myself. I haven't had time to tidy, but as it's been just me these last couple of days, it's really not too bad. A bit dusty, maybe. "Would you like a glass?"

"I'd love some red, please, if you're joining me."

"Yes, it seems like a red day. Nice and warming, with the awful weather." *Oh god, oh god, stop talking about the weather.*

We go through to the kitchen, and I open the bottle and pour us both a glass. I hand Tony his and he takes it, then puts his arm around my waist and pulls me in for a kiss. It sets us both at ease, somehow, and as we pull apart, we smile.

"Cheers, Maggie," he says, pushing his glass lightly against mine.

"Cheers. Are you hungry?"

"I am, as it happens. Here, let me help. We can get it done in half the time."

He prepares the salad, while I toss the halloumi in cornflour mixed with paprika, salt and black pepper, then heat the pan to fry it.

While I plate up, he takes the cutlery, our wine glasses, and the bottle, through to the table.

We tuck into our food quietly, that strange semi-shyness settling over us again. And the longer we are quiet, the harder it is to think of something to say, which won't sound forced, or like I'm just trying to break the silence. It feels funny sitting here with him, and not my daughter.

"Are you missing Stevie?" he asks, as if reading my mind.

"I am," I admit. "It's strange. I mean, it's good she's with Mum. I know she's really missed her. And I am really enjoying work, but it does feel weird. It really does."

I want to ask him if he wanted, or still wants, kids. I want to know why he and his ex didn't have any, though I know it's not a pre-requisite, of anything. I think of Julia, who has only so recently discovered she wants to be a mum. Not everyone wants to be a parent. But if Tony has no interest in children, how does that work for me and him?

I am jumping ahead, as usual.

I take a sip of my wine, and a surreptitious glance at Tony. I don't even know exactly how old he is, I realise. I know he's older than me. In his forties, I think. But men can have kids any time, can't they? Look at Des O'Connor. What if Tony does want kids? I don't really think I want any more. Maybe there was a time when I might have, but now Stevie is growing up and I'm just finding my feet, and rediscovering my own sense of self.

Jumping ahead, again.

"I'm so pleased you like the job, Maggie. I knew you'd be perfect for it. Even if I… we.. hadn't…"

I smile. "It's a bit of an odd situation, isn't it?"

"Yes, I suppose. It's… do you mind?"

"No. I don't. I think if we were working for the same company, it might be a bit weird. I think I'd feel self-conscious."

"I know what you mean. We put on our work personas a bit, don't we? Which doesn't mean they're not really us. But they're just a part of us. One of our faces. I did… I was dating somebody I worked with. Before you, I mean. It wasn't anything serious, or not from my perspective. Oh god, I sound a right bastard, don't I? It was just… I really respected her. Still do. She's so good at what she does. And everyone at work's scared of her. She's… formidable. When we went out a few times, I saw a completely different side of her. A vulnerability. She'd hate it if I said that, I'm sure. I hope you don't mind me talking about this? I think I'm just trying to say that who we are at work doesn't necessarily equal who we really are. And I know it takes an extra effort sometimes, to find the confidence we need to speak up. It's almost like acting. So if the person you're in a relationship with is there, it can feel difficult, and like they know you're not being yourself."

I nod. "That's exactly it. It's hard enough to suggest ideas sometimes, and I think I'd find it harder to do in front of you." In the background, I'm thinking *'A relationship'… I think he just called what we have a relationship.*

I pop the last piece of halloumi into my mouth just as my phone starts buzzing in the kitchen. I don't want to get it. It seems rude. But it rings off, and then starts again, so I go through to pick it up.

"It's Stevie," I say apologetically.

"Answer it! Don't stand on ceremony for me." He smiles. I smile back. I want to go to him and kiss him. But I don't.

"Hi, love," I say.

"Mum?" I can tell immediately that something is wrong. "Can you come? It's Grandma. She's hurt."

"Hurt?" I exclaim, and see Tony look at me sharply. "What's wrong with her?"

"She went outside and got hit by something, on the head. And the leg."

"What was she doing outside…?" I say, then, "Never mind. I'm coming. Does she need an ambulance? Is she conscious?"

"No. I mean, yes, she is conscious. And she says she doesn't need an ambulance. But she's bleeding. And she's being a bit weird."

"What kind of weird? No, don't answer that. I'm on my way. Just sit tight, OK? And call me if she gets any worse."

"I'm so sorry," I say to Tony after I've hung up. "It's my mum. I think she's hurt. Stevie says she's been hit by something, and is being weird. I don't know. Maybe it's nothing. But I'd better go."

"I'll take you," he says. "No objections. Let's go."

So we lock up the house and run through the gusts of wind and now hammering rain, to his car. I'm breathing hard, and so is he, as we pull the doors closed.

"Let's go," he says. "You can put the postcode in the satnav, or just tell me how to get there. OK?"

"OK." I say in a small voice.

"Sorry. I feel like I've just become very bossy! I just want to help, I promise. I'll get you to your mum's and wait in the car, OK? And you can let me know if I can help, or if you want me to bugger off."

"Thank you, Tony." I smile, and he puts his hand briefly on my knee. He has lovely hands, with tiny dark hairs on the back of them. But now is not the time for admiring Tony's hands.

I check my phone. Message Stevie.

**We're on our way xxx**

I feel small, and scared, not just of what might have happened to Mum, but also of this storm, which throws itself at the side of the car once we're out of the shelter of town and on the more exposed roads. There is not a lot of other traffic; I know there was bravado about the severity of British weather, but actually this is as bad as I've ever known a summer storm to be. All along the route, there is debris strewn across pavements and driveways, in the road. Tony drives very slowly, to avoid it, which I appreciate, but I'm also wishing he'd go faster, to get me to my mum. There are trees with broken branches – thankfully none making the roads impassable, but scary to think what would happen if one fell on the car – and blown-over bins; the contents of recycling boxes, and indeed some of the boxes themselves, skidding along giddily. A pub A-frame sign is lying in the road, which is flooded in places, too, and the tents in the campsite we pass look like they've been trampled by a giant. The poor people staying there. Hopefully they've managed to find shelter somewhere. Tony's windscreen wipers go ten to the dozen as he tries to keep visibility.

Once we reach the relative safety of the next town, the rain has died off a little, but the wind shows no signs of easing up. The sea is a deep, churning, angry grey, like it's heating to boiling point, when it might bubble right over and swallow the town.

Tony navigates the narrow streets, and pulls up outside Mum's building. There is a small car port there, and I don't know if it's for next door or what, but he says he'll wait there, and I should just let him know if he can help. I smile gratefully, then dash out of the car, to hammer on the door to Mum's flat. My heart is beating wildly, as I wonder what I'll find inside.

# 1996

As the end of fifth year approached, Maggie began to feel very strange, like somebody was pulling the rug very slowly from underneath her feet. Throughout her life, she had been given to moments of panic, normally induced by change. It had been hard moving to Cornwall from Bristol, but she'd done it, and she'd felt settled at school, and at home. Now, exams loomed, and then an extra-long summer, before college, and who knew what.

She had opted to go to a different college, away from the school, while Julia and Stacey both wanted to stay at the school sixth form. It was something a little bit stubborn in her, Maggie thought, but also she knew she wanted a change. To be herself, and not live in the shadow of her more popular sister and friend. Whether or not Julia and Stacey really were more popular than Maggie was up for debate, but it was how she felt. She wanted to start afresh, where there were new people who would take her at face value.

Now that the time was coming closer, though, she was experiencing cold feet. Was it really such a good idea? To leave a place where she now felt so comfortable, with fellow pupils, and teachers, she already knew? The thought of starting afresh, stepping into the unknown, had begun to make her feel sick. There were only a handful of others going off to the college alongside her, but one of them was Mark Beaumont, which was definitely a point in its favour.

Mark was her science partner, and secret crush. Well, not secret to Julia or Stacey, of course, but he had no idea – or at least she hoped he didn't. They got on well, and Mark had become a regular visitor to the Cavendish house. Jeff and Lucy really liked him, although Lucy feared she could see only too well where this was heading. She sensed Maggie's feelings towards Mark, but also sensed that Mark's own feelings, though perfectly genuine, were not of the romantic kind. He had bought Maggie a beautiful pen for her birthday, and Maggie's face had flushed with delight when she'd opened it.

"I'd say he's pretty keen," Jeff said, when Lucy voiced her fears to him.

"Yes, I think he is, but not necessarily in the way Maggie would like," Lucy said. Still, she had been through it all herself – the teenage years; the broken heart, unrequited love, the works – and she had survived. It was something that had to be endured, and probably helped to shape a better, stronger person in the long run. She couldn't protect her daughters from everything; and may not be doing them a favour if she did. Instead, she would just have to be there for Maggie if and when her daughter needed her. And maybe she would be proven wrong, anyway.

There was a big party planned for the end of the school year, once every last exam paper booklet had been closed and collected, and the teachers had breathed a sigh of relief and waved their erstwhile pupils a sometimes fond, and sometimes grateful, goodbye.

The venue was a clearing in the woods not far from the twins' house, and the kids from school were coming in small groups, clutching bottles of cider and ten-packs of Marlboro red or Benson & Hedges. Many of them had their sights set on a particular member of the opposite – or occasionally the same – sex. Some of them had their sights set on anyone who would have them. The air was full of anticipation and excitement. The class of 96 were coming of age.

Robert Bastion was there, as always with Paul Cooper and James Watson. Their friendship had stood the test of time, and Maggie and Robert were quite good friends these days. She couldn't imagine why she had been interested in him, though, and thought that these days Stacey would be quite welcome to him.

Stacey, meanwhile, had been going out with an older lad for some time, but he'd recently finished with her. He had a car, or at least access to a car, and he'd taken her off to many a party, and – she claimed – even a few raves, so this little gathering might have been deemed beneath her, but she was as excited as any of the others.

She was wearing a low-cut top, with a black leather biker jacket that Maggie was pretty sure was Sarah's, and very short denim cut-offs, and she was of course drawing a lot of attention to herself, holding court with a small group of girls, waving a cigarette in the air, and necking cider like it was going out of fashion.

Julia, Maggie noticed, seemed to quickly distance herself from Stacey, and in fact made a bit of a beeline for Paul Cooper, the boy she had danced with at that first Christmas disco. Nothing had ever happened between the two of them, after they had exchanged Christmas presents, and Julia had been out with a few boys over the years, but Maggie knew Julia had always had a soft spot for Paul.

It seemed the feeling was mutual. He smiled at Julia as she approached, and offered her his can of beer. Julia shook her head, but accepted his cigarette, which shocked Maggie. She herself was not one for smoking, but had brought a small bottle of vodka, which she had tipped away a little of to make room for some lime cordial.

As she looked around the growing group of kids, she unscrewed the lid from the bottle and took a swig. Urgh. It was sort of sweet, and sort of like nail polish remover – not that she had ever tasted that, but she imagined it might be a little like vodka. She took another swig, however, to calm her nerves, and looked around for Mark. It didn't take long to spot him, and she waved. He smiled and came over.

"Maggie!" he said.

"Hello. Want some?" She proffered her bottle.

"What is it?"

"Vodka and lime."

"Go on, then… urgh!" He pulled a face. "You like that stuff?"

"Not really," she admitted, and they both laughed.

"Looks like Paul and Julia are getting on well," he smiled, and stepped aside slightly, to reveal Maggie's twin sister and Paul sitting together under a tree, and kissing.

"Had to happen sometime," Maggie said, in what she hoped was a cool manner.

"I guess!" Mark smiled.

"So…"

"So…" he echoed.

Maggie took another swig of drink. Mark was

standing tantalisingly close. She could just move her hand and be holding his. But she couldn't… could she?

"Mark!" she heard, and they both turned to see his best friend, Tony, calling him over to a group of lads, who were trying to build a fire. "Come on, mate, you're good at this stuff."

"Back in a bit," Mark said, apologetically, and Maggie felt her heart lift.

Then, "Make or break time for you two, eh?" She heard Stacey's voice behind her.

"Oh, hi, Stacey. What do you mean?"

"You and Marky boy!"

"Erm…"

"Looks like Julia's pulled, anyway. Mind if I…?" she gestured to Maggie's bottle.

"No, I…"

Stacey took the little bottle, unscrewed it, and took a huge swig. "Not bad," she said, wiping her mouth. At the same moment, there were whoops from the bunch of boys Mark had gone over to.

"Nice one, Mark!" Tony was saying, as they stood back to watch the flames take hold. It wasn't a great idea, thought Maggie, to have a fire in the open, and hadn't there been stories of wildfires started just this way, quickly destroying woodland and farmland that had dried out in the summer heat? But she wouldn't dare say anything. And besides, she couldn't help but feel a little bit proud that Mark had started it.

It didn't take long for the party to get out of hand, or at least for some of the party-goers to get a bit over-excited. The combination of a summer of freedom, the end of school as they knew it, and being unused to the various cheap and nasty alcoholic drinks they had brought along with them – some stolen from parents' drinks cabinets, some bought for them by older siblings, or down-with-it parents, and some bought courtesy of fake IDs – took its toll. Soon there was more than one casualty.

It began, predictably, with Jason Norris, who not many people had really wanted to invite, on account of his obnoxious loudness, and tendency to overdo it where alcohol was concerned. He had been one of the group of lads who had got into trouble tombstoning the previous summer. They had been drinking, and decided to take the plunge at a notorious spot. They had not taken account of the tide, and that the water was at the time fairly shallow. One of his friends had been airlifted to hospital, having shattered one of his legs, and damaged his spine. The others had been taken off to the local police station for a dressing down, but it appeared to have made little difference.

The next victim, surprisingly, was James Watson. Maggie spotted him leaning against a tree. Robert and the rest of them were nearby – well, the rest of them except for Paul Cooper (and Julia was also missing, Maggie realised) – and they were laughing at their friend. Maggie glared at them, and went over to James. She didn't know if she had ever seen anybody look so pale.

"Are you OK?" she asked.

"Urgh, no, I…" He was holding his stomach.

"Have you been sick?"

"No, but…" It seemed like just the word 'sick' was

142

enough to make him heave, and within a moment, he was doubled over. "Maggie," he managed between vomits, "I'm so embarrassed. Please, don't stay over here while I'm like this."

"I'm going nowhere," she said, firmly, although scanning the crowd for Mark. There he was, still by the fire, which had quite a few kids round it now. Somebody was handing Mark a guitar. She had no idea he played. It just made him all the more perfect.

"I mean it."

"No, I'm staying here, just till you're done throwing up. Then we can go to the phone box, and call your mum and dad."

"Don't do that!" he wailed. "I'll be alright, honestly. They'll go mad if they see me like this. I'm staying at Rob's tonight."

"OK." Maggie stood tall and walked up to the group of boys where Robert was holding court. "You'd better look after James," she said. "If he's coming back to yours. Make sure he gets back safely."

"Why are you so concerned?" Robert grinned infuriatingly, and a flicker of laughter ran around the group of boys. "Got a vested interest, have you?"

"No. He's just a good friend, and a nice person. And he shouldn't have been drinking so much."

"He's hardly had anything!" Scott Nicholson scoffed. "He's just a lightweight."

"Well, so what? What does that matter? Just look after him, OK?" She didn't even look at Scott, but addressed Rob.

"I will," he said, and she couldn't tell if he was mocking her. How had she ever found him attractive?

The sooner she moved on to college, and uni, the better. "Hadn't you better be looking out for your sister, anyway?" he asked.

There was another round of chuckles, and a wolf-whistle.

"Haven't you noticed she's gone off into the trees with Paul?"

So that's where Julia was! This seemed so out of character. But then again, not many of the kids here were acting their normal selves. And Maggie felt fairly sure that Paul wasn't going to do anything out of order. He had liked Julia since day one of first year, and he'd only ever been polite and friendly to both of the girls. So Julia had gone into the woods with him. So what? She was sixteen years old. It wasn't anything different to what lots of girls their age were doing.

Right, she thought. Time for herself, now, or she would miss her own opportunity. She was aware of some guitar music, and singing from around the fire. The light was fading a little amidst the trees, as the sun had sunk lower in the sky. She put her hand in her bag, for her bottle. Having seen the effects of alcohol on James, she knew she wasn't going to drink much, but she fancied a little spot of Dutch courage, as she was sure she'd heard it called. She was going to find Mark, and, and... and what? Ask him out? Kiss him? She didn't know. But also, she couldn't find her bottle of vodka. She looked behind her. Had it fallen out of her bag? Maybe it wasn't such a bad thing, she thought.

As she approached the group around the fire, however, she saw the bottle... in the hands of Stacey, who waved it at her. "Not much left!" she called cheerfully. "We've been a bit greedy, haven't we, Mark?"

And yes, of course, as Maggie might have known, Stacey was sitting with Mark Beaumont. Not just with him, but leaning right up against him. And he was no longer playing the guitar, but reclining against a log, looking quite drunk. He had a stupid grin on his face, thought Maggie, who was sober as a judge. The look did not suit him, she thought, primly.

"You've… how did you get that?" Maggie asked, unable to keep the annoyance from her voice.

"You gave it to me!" Stacey said, and laughed.

"When…? Oh… Well, you shouldn't have just kept it. Or you could have kept it safe for me."

"I have kept it safe! Well, *we* have, haven't we, Mark?" Stacey snaked her arm around Mark's neck. He did nothing to stop her. Maggie felt her heart begin to crack. When Stacey pulled Mark's head around and kissed him, the crack became a chasm, and she turned on her heel and fled. Past James Watson, who was back with his friends, looking remarkably perkier, and called out to her. She didn't reply. Past Julia and Paul, who were emerging hand-in-hand from the woods, looking very smug and pleased with themselves, Maggie thought. Out of the woods, into the open, where the sky suddenly opened up, and some daylight returned. She took a moment to stop, and catch her breath. She wanted to cry, but she didn't. She was too angry with her supposed friend, and with herself, for being such a fool. And disappointed in Mark, for being so bloody weak. And obvious. Only a boy with no imagination would fall for Stacey's supposed charms. But that meant he was not the boy she'd thought.

This was it, then. The end of school. She had two years at college, and she was sure now that she'd made the right choice, to go somewhere different, and leave all of this behind her. And then uni... and the wider world.

She was pleased for Julia, as Paul was a nice boy, but it still smarted that she herself had never had a boyfriend. Not so much as kissed a boy, to be quite honest – if you didn't count during a game of spin the bottle, when she and James Watson kept getting each other, and it had begun to feel embarrassing, so she had said she needed the toilet, and left the game.

As she walked home through the dusk, birdsong lifting on the air, she felt bad for leaving Julia, but she was fairly sure that Paul would see her sister home. She knew that Jeff and Lucy were out with friends, so she could wallow for a little while, in her bad luck, and overall disappointment in life.

As Maggie opened the door, she was met by an over-excited Pretzel, who leaped at her, licking her face, and making her laugh. But then she was crying. "Oh, Pretzel," she said. "Oh, Pretzel." And she sank down against the wall, letting him lick the salty tears from her face. But even then, somehow, from somewhere, she could feel a strength beginning to flood into her. Tinged with self-pity, maybe, but strength nevertheless. She had been let down, yes, and not for the first time. And maybe nobody had ever fancied her, and nobody ever would. The thought was scary, but she swallowed it back. It wasn't the be-all and end-all, was it? She, Maggie Cavendish, was a feminist, and she was damned if she was going to be judged on how attractive she was. That was for Stacey, Maggie thought bitchily. She didn't have much else to offer, after all.

As she leaned her forehead against Pretzel's, Maggie resolved that she would not give in. She would not let Stacey see how hurt she was, and she would not trust that girl again. This was it, she thought. She would go on to college, and then she would leave this little town behind. Today might mark the end of something, but it was also a new beginning.

# Maggie

"Mum!" When she sees me, Stevie looks like she might burst into tears.

"Are you OK?" I hug her quickly. "Is Mum? Where is she?"

"I'm here, Maggie." I'm relieved to hear Mum's voice. I hurry through to the living room, where Mum is sitting on the settee, her left leg up on a table and a bloody-looking tea towel pressed to her head.

"Mum! Are you alright?" I ask, thinking what a stupid question that is. "What happened?"

"Oh, it's my own fault, really. I was taking a bin bag out. I should have just waited till the storm had blown over. Anyway, I got clonked on the head by a flying bin lid – the wind just caught it, and it cracked me right here–" she lifts the tea towel a little gingerly – "and then I lost my footing on the slippery steps, and twisted my ankle. I might have banged my head again, I think. It's quite sore. I'm sorry, I didn't know Stevie had called you, she only just told me."

I feel relief flood through me. "Thank god for that!"

"Gave you a bit of a scare, Stevie, I think. I'm sorry," Mum says, squeezing Stevie's hand.

"You said Mum was acting a bit…" I prompt Stevie, not wanting to say too much.

"Weird. She was. You were, Granny," she insists.

"Was I, my love? I'm sorry. I did go a bit woozy, for a while."

"What do you mean by woozy?"

"Oh, just light-headed. I think it might have been the sight of the blood," she says ruefully. "I'm a bit squeamish."

"You're not!" I say.

"I am. I never told you. Don't you remember, it was always your dad who patched you and Julia up, if I could avoid it?"

I think back. Maybe I do remember that. I'd never really thought of it before. "Well, let me take a look at you, help get you cleaned up," I say. "I used to be a first-aider at work, you know. Hopefully I can remember a thing or two."

While I'm cleaning the cut on Mum's head – which thankfully looks superficial, but I think will leave her with quite a bruise, Mum says, "I am sorry you had to come out in this dreadful weather," Mum says. "Did you park nearby?"

"I – I got a lift."

"A lift? With whom?"

"A... friend. From work."

"And where is she now?" Mum sits forward, concerned. She's always been one for thinking of others.

"*He...* is outside," I say. "He just wanted to wait to make sure everything's OK. I'll go down in a few minutes and tell him he can go."

"You don't have to stay, Maggie," Mum says.

"It's fine. Honestly." A sudden gust of wind rushes against the house, making the windows shake.

"Will your friend be alright, travelling back in this

weather?" she asks doubtfully. I know my mum, and I can see a decision is being made. "Invite him in," she says. "Go on. It's awful out there, and there's plenty of room in here. He can't go driving back in this weather. If anything happened to him, I'd feel awful. Stevie, would you be a love and put the kettle on, please?"

"Of course." Stevie looks glad to have something to do, and scuttles out of the room.

"Just a friend, is it?" Mum looks at me slyly, and I can see she's perfectly herself.

"Yes, Mum," I say, in a mock-teenage way, but I can't help grinning widely.

She is right. I can't very well send Tony back in this weather. And I can't leave him sitting in his car. I take a deep breath and go downstairs to invite him in. Some of my carefully constructed little worlds are about to collide, but it doesn't feel quite as scary as I'd thought it might.

# 1998

Keeping to her plan, Maggie got three A* A-Levels, and secured a place at all the universities she had applied to. She had kept her friendship with Mark Beaumont, although it was never quite the same. Julia had told her that he had in fact rejected Stacey that night of the end of school party, even as Maggie was leaving. Apparently, he'd told her he wasn't interested, calling it 'futile', which Maggie thought sounded a bit condescending, and she almost caught herself feeling sorry for Stacey. She might have taken Mark's rejection of Stacey as a sign that she should try again, but she had been so angry, and so let down, that she had made up her mind, and she kept it firmly on her studies. In time, Mark started going out with Lacey, who had gone to a different school to them, and his and Maggie's friendship all but fizzled out.

Bristol seemed the obvious choice to Maggie, and so she accepted her place there, studying psychology and English literature, finding a room in the halls of residence near the Downs, and taking the time to link back up with some of her old friends, who she and Julia had kept loosely in touch with over the years – but of course most of them were going off on adventures of their own: other towns, other unis, or even gap-year travelling.

Still, it felt good to be somewhere so familiar, and yet so different. And to meet her new course mates and hall residents not as a twin, but as an absolute individual. She could be who she wanted to be.

And it was fun, so much fun, with all the parties and

nights out clubbing, or parties in different blocks. She had the advantage of having previously lived in the city and, although she couldn't remember all that many places, she could pass herself off as being pretty knowledgeable and experienced. She made friends quickly, and soon found out that she wasn't destined to be Julia's ugly sister forever. She found some boys liked her, and she liked some of them back. Some of them wanted to play the field, and she wasn't into that idea. It wasn't her, really. So she took her time, and got to know a boy on her course, who in time asked her out, and she said yes. Adrian had spent a year travelling around Europe with his friends, and he seemed so worldly to Maggie. He was full of stories of adventures, and she would hang on his every word, wishing she had been with him. He was kind, and smart, and worked hard, and he may not have set her heart alight, but she was over all that. He was a good person, and she was happy to be with him.

The two of them would walk across the Downs together, and down Whiteladies Road, all the way to the university buildings near the Victoria Rooms and the Triangle, and Dingles department store. Maggie loved walking across the grass in the mornings, following and followed by scores of other students, all trying to conserve money by not getting the bus. Whether cold or warm, it was a lovely walk, as long as it was dry. In the rain and the wind, it was a different matter, and she did occasionally splash out on a bus fare, when the weather was really bad. It wouldn't do to spend a day in lectures soaking wet.

She would speak to her parents and Julia once or

twice a week. Julia had stayed in Cornwall, and decided to get a job at a big school of dance, doing a mixture of admin and teaching support. She'd enjoyed sixth form, but lost interest in studying.

Stacey was out of the picture entirely, having moved back up to Yorkshire sometime during lower sixth, after Sarah had decided to get married again, and Stacey had decided to go and live with her dad. Maggie never heard from her anymore. It was no great loss, she thought.

Julia was still going out with Paul. He was now at uni in Exeter, and travelled back to Cornwall every weekend to see Julia. Maggie wouldn't have been surprised if they ended up marrying. She loved her twin, but felt further apart from her with each passing month, as their lives and interests seemed to be going in such different directions. It felt like they had less in common these days, and that made her sad.

The first Christmas she returned home, she barely saw Julia, who was either out with Paul, at Paul's family home, or had invited Paul to theirs. Maggie was glad enough to see him, but she felt slightly pushed out. And, even though she had only been in Bristol for two months, it felt like she had already missed out on a lot at home, and like her parents and her sister were closer than ever. She perhaps was making herself feel like that, but it drove her on, in her determination, to make a success of her life. She told herself she didn't want to settle for a local boy, like her sister had, and see nothing of the world, but if she was very honest, she was a little bit jealous, and a little insecure.

In the second year, when Adrian asked her if she'd like to spend Christmas with him and his family, in Birmingham, she thought about it, and said yes. She knew Lucy and Jeff would be hurt, but they had Paul and Julia now. And she didn't want to offend Adrian or his parents, either. She had been to visit a couple of times, and when Adrian's mum and dad had been in Bristol they'd taken her out to the theatre and for a meal with them. It all felt very grown up, and sophisticated.

On Christmas Day, though, Maggie found herself wishing she had thought it through. She had never had a Christmas when she and Julia had not woken up and opened their stockings together, giggling over the traditional underwear, socks and silly toys, and stuffing their mouths with Terry's Chocolate Orange slices. At Adrian's, it was a very different affair, with no stockings, and a staid breakfast of croissants, preserves and coffee in the dining room, while Maggie knew back home Lucy or Jeff would be whipping up pancakes in the kitchen and the room would be bright and warm and full of laughter. She felt on edge and unable to relax and she held back tears when they put on the CD of Carols from Kings, as she thought of her family, and Pretzel, who might be missing her and wondering why she had not been home for so long. She sat through the present-opening ritual, and thanked Adrian's parents for her leather gloves, and box of expensive chocolates, politely exclaiming at their gifts to each other. And at lunchtime, Adrian's sister Sophia came over with her husband David and their children, Timothy and Ariella. Maggie had not met them before, and found herself quite tongue-tied, even with the children, who seemed unnaturally well-behaved to her.

In the afternoon, she went for a walk with Adrian and told him she would be going to Cornwall the next day.

"Why?" he had asked, his face full of concern. "Have I upset you?"

"No!" she had kissed him, liking his kindness. "But it's a family time, isn't it? And this is your family, but mine are in Cornwall. And I miss them."

"Oh. I understand," he'd said, but he had seemed sad. She hadn't wanted him to be sad, but she also had not wanted to stay with him and his quiet, well-meaning, but unfamiliar family.

Jeff, Lucy and Julia were delighted when she arrived, unannounced, on Boxing Day evening. There were cheers, hugs, kisses, and maybe even a tear or two. Pretzel was beside himself. Paul was, predictably, there as well, but he also seemed happy to see her. "She's missed you, you know," he said, gesturing towards Julia, when he had the chance to.

"Has she?"

"Of course!"

Maggie realised how much she had missed her sister, too. And her parents. Her home. Her messy, happy, noisy home. She went to bed happier than she had been for some time, the only thing niggling at the back of her mind was that she was going to have to find a way to finish with Adrian.

When it was time to return to Bristol, Maggie knew she'd be back home the following Christmas. And that she would be single. It was studying for her from now on, although not entirely without a few good nights out and parties. She loved living in the city. She could walk into town, to the docks, or up to the Downs. There were pubs, and clubs, and cinemas, and shops. And so many businesses where she thought she might like to work. Cornwall would always be home, but she couldn't imagine going back to live there.

When she graduated, she took on a house share with two of her friends, Angela and Mali, who also wanted to stay, and they went down to sign up with the myriad temping agencies, getting a range of short-term admin jobs. Maggie was stationed at the head office of a charity, where she was soon offered a permanent job, and quickly came to understand the way the place worked. She found her colleagues were mostly friendly and sociable, and began to have regular Friday-night drinks with them, catching the late bus back to her house share, or walking home with her housemates if they'd come to join her. She loved to walk up St Michael's Hill, and see the lights of the city at night. It was loud, and full of life, and just what she needed. It suited her slightly stubborn streak, to be somewhere so different to Cornwall.

Sometimes, Julia would come for the weekend, with or without Paul, and Maggie loved to take her sister out, introducing her to a life she had never lived. Paul and Julia had got engaged not long after he returned from university and took a role in his family business. They were saving for a house, wanting somewhere to live, before they got married. Julia seemed happy, so Maggie was pleased for them, but she would not have swapped her life for theirs, not at that stage. She was having far too much fun, most of the time.

She was also seeing Andy, a colleague from work, who was older than her, and separated from his wife. She had no doubt that this relationship was not destined for success, but there was something nice about being with somebody more experienced and mature (at least that was how he had seemed at the time).

In the summer, Maggie would take two weeks off work and return to her family home. It was a welcome relief, from the day-in, day-out bus rides to the city centre, and eight hours at a desk. She had two weeks of freedom, to get in the sea every day, and while away the hours reading on the beach, or in the garden. Jeff and Lucy and Julia were always there, always the same, and always so pleased to see her. No matter what she told herself, she missed her home, and her family, and it always took her a few days to get back into the swing of things when she returned to Bristol.

One year, she returned home to find Pretzel a shadow of his former self, and the four of them made the decision together that the vet should put him to sleep. It was awful, and more than once Maggie worried that they had done the wrong thing, and questioned whether they should really have that power to decide over life and death. But his legs had all but given way under him, and he was sad and subdued. It was the right thing, she was sure, but it didn't hurt any less.

When she returned to Bristol this time, she finished with Andy, and applied for the role of PA to the charity director. She was offered the job on the spot, and was suddenly earning twice as much money as she had been before, and decided to find her own place. She had loved the house-share, but it was time to take the next step in her life. Julia and Paul were due to marry the following summer, and Maggie knew that she ought to be growing up, too.

# Maggie

"This is lovely, Mum," I say. I've always wanted to have a meal at Tregynon Manor, the posh hotel on the edge of town, but funds have never allowed. Mum has insisted on treating me and Tony, though.

"Honestly, you put your own safety aside to come rushing to my aid!" she said.

It seems a little melodramatic, put like that, but I'm not complaining. The hotel is absolutely beautiful – and just as Elise described. I find myself imagining how she felt, seeing the place for the first time as a young girl – for this was where her school was evacuated to during the war. And then she ended up working here, as a governess, when the war was over, and the family returned. I find it incredible to think of all that she has seen in her lifetime, and how much things have changed. Stevie sits next to Mum, looking at her phone. She's not much older than Elise was when she first came here. I bet those girls were made to sit incredibly politely and properly at mealtimes. Imagine if they'd known about the digital revolution that was coming their way! And how kids these days – and adults, too – often sit at the table with their eyes glued to their screens, scrolling through endless drivel. I'm not judging. I am just as bad. I'm terrible for running through post after post on the local Facebook community page, and it's a guilty pleasure to read through the comments, too – some making me laugh, others making my blood boil. However, I do draw the line at sitting at the table with a phone, and Stevie knows this.

"Ahem," I say to her.

She looks up, entirely unmoved. "I'm just trying to find some photos for Granny," she says, "from the trampoline place."

"Hmm," I say.

"I am!" She is outraged, and I am treated to a little image of the teenage battles we no doubt have to come.

We have three empty seats at the table. Tony is on his way, as are Paul and Julia. They're coming down for Mum's last week here, and have booked into a B&B on the next street down from where she's staying. I'm so excited about seeing my sister again. It's a special thing, being a twin. I realise that more and more.

The waitress brings over some menus for us and takes our drinks orders.

"I'll have a gin & tonic, please."

"And I'll have the same," Mum smiles. "Stevie? What are you having?"

"An orange juice, please, Grandma." The waitress heads to the bar while Stevie pushes her phone across to Mum and then looks up, over my shoulder. "Auntie Julia!"

I turn, and stand up, to see Julia and Paul grinning from ear to ear. Julia envelops me in a huge hug first. "Maggie. I've missed you so much."

"I've missed you, too. Like you wouldn't believe. Sit next to me, will you?"

"Er – of course!"

I'd issued the request before thinking of Tony. It's a bit of a baptism of fire, I think, this first family meal. But he and Mum got on like a house on fire, and he was lovely with Stevie. Once I'd invited him in out of the wind and rain, he'd gone to shake Mum's hand, but she'd pulled him in for a hug. He'd offered Stevie his hand – "Anthony Jones. Pleased to meet you," he'd said, extremely formally, which made her laugh. Mum, with more colour in her cheeks than when I'd arrived, but with her leg still up on the stool, soon had me opening a bottle of wine, and later another. We played board games with Stevie, and watched from the windows as the sky grew fully dark, and the wind and the rain threw tantrum after tantrum against the windows, the doors, the walls, the palm tree in the garden outside, and all over town, but generally failed to get their own way. I gather that the combination of high tide and the storm resulted in some flooding of the road along the harbourside, but nothing too dramatic, and all the businesses there were well prepared, with sandbags which happily did the job this time.

At about ten o'clock, Stevie fell asleep on the sofa, and I gently woke her to lead her into her bedroom, then Mum showed Tony and me to the spare room, and tactfully went to her bed herself. Not before whispering, "He's lovely!" to me while she was piling towels onto my arms in the hallway.

"I know!" I couldn't help but feel a rush of excitement and joy, at having brought her and Tony together, and it being such a success.

So now it's their second meeting, and I'm nervous

now as to how he and Julia and Paul will get along. Paul places himself next to Stevie, so that when Tony arrives he has no choice but to sit next to my sister, and opposite her husband. It is near enough impossible for me to talk to him, I realise. I hope he's OK.

"You're not going to interrogate him, are you?" I murmur to Julia while Tony is exchanging pleasantries with Paul.

"No! Of course not. But I do need to know that he's a suitable match for you. I've just got a few questions…"

"Julia!" I laugh, warningly. She has never really known anyone I've been in a relationship with – just the occasional meeting when she'd visited me in Bristol.

"Only kidding. I feel nervous!" she says.

"What have you got to feel nervous about?"

"What if he doesn't like me? Mum says he's really into you, so I need to make a good impression."

"Did Mum really say that?"

"Yes! Well, I don't think she said 'into you'. More like, 'Your sister's suitor is clearly besotted.'" She puts on an upper-middle-class kind of voice.

Mum calls across the table, "You're not making fun of me, are you?"

"As if!" we chorus. How does she know?

Soon enough, we are eating our starters, and my second gin & tonic is helping me to feel at ease. I'm so happy to be here, with my family. So happy to have Julia next to me. And so happy to see Tony sitting with us all, as if he completely belongs. Stevie and Paul are deep in conversation, as are Tony and Julia. I needn't have worried. Not everybody gets as tied in nervous knots as I do. Tony has plenty to say, but is a good listener, too. I hear him asking Julia about her dance school, and her expanding on how difficult it can be, but how much she loves it. I realise I barely ask her about her work these days, and haven't for some time. It's quite an achievement, what she's created with that school, and I know it can't always be easy. I make a mental note to show more interest.

It all feels so natural. I don't want this meal to end. But, of course, it must. As we're getting our things together, and waiting for the waitress to bring Mum's card back, Mum looks across the table and smiles at me. I feel suddenly, gut-wrenchingly sad that she'll be going home next week.

"Alright?" she asks.

"Yes," I say. "Just… happy. But thinking I'm going to miss you."

"Well," she says, "I wanted to talk to you about that…"

But we are interrupted by a voice from behind me. "Maggie! I thought it was you!"

I turn to see Elise, and Ada behind her.

"Hello!" I say, standing to greet her, and hurriedly remembering what she thinks she knows about my family. "Hi Ada," I say as well. "Back again!"

"Ada!" Stevie says, excitedly. Her face flushes with excitement. "Uncle Paul, this is my friend I was telling you about."

Paul smiles, and says hello, and Stevie pushes past him, so she can run round to give Ada a hug. She's over-excited by it all, and it does make me smile, but I know I am going to have to make some introductions. "Elise," I say, "this is my Mum, Lucy – and my sister, Julia."

"I can see you're sisters," says Elise. "Lovely to meet

you, Julia." I see her eyes cast around the table, no doubt wondering where Julia's three sons are. "And you as well, Lucy."

Am I imagining things, or are Elise's shrewd eyes assessing Mum? Thinking that she's not how she'd thought she would be. Because Mum is lovely, and I would say that's obvious to anyone. Her years of friendly, pleasant, kind and caring behaviour shine through – in her eyes, and just the set of her face. Little crinkly lines around her eyes, and a slight crease at the corners of her mouth, which suggest she is always about to smile, if she isn't already. She greets Elise with an open smile.

"And this is Paul, Julia's husband," I say, turning to my brother-in-law, who sees that my cheeks are flushed, and is looking at me with his eyebrows slightly raised. I finally turn to the person who I know Elise is most curious to meet. "And this is Tony."

To her credit, Elise does not react any differently. "I'm pleased to meet all of you," she says. "And how funny to see you here. Louisa's insisted on bringing us for lunch today… she'll be here any minute, she was just outside, taking a work call."

"I'll keep an eye out for her on our way out. And I'll come and see you one afternoon next week if that's OK – we can both come, can't we, Stevie?"

"Yes. Will you still be here, Ada?"

"I'm afraid not," Elise's lovely granddaughter smiles. "But I'll be back at Christmas. If not before. And you're coming to see us in London, aren't you, Grandma?"

"Yes!" Elise beams. "I thought I'd better have one more trip to the old place."

"Erm, I don't know about 'one more'," Ada says. "The first of many, more like."

"We'll see!" Elise takes her granddaughter's arm. "Enjoy the rest of your stay, Lucy. Your daughter's a lovely girl."

"She certainly is," says Mum. "They both are."

"Mu-um," both Julia and I chorus, like teenagers, and it makes everyone laugh.

We leave the restaurant, a happy group, full of good food, good drink, and good cheer. "How about a walk on the beach to blow the cobwebs away?" I suggest.

"Good idea," says Mum.

I am arm-in-arm with Julia and Mum, while Stevie chatters away to Tony and Paul right behind us. We traipse around the corner, to head down the hill towards the beach, and walk headlong into Elise's daughter, Louisa.

"Oh, hi," she says, her phone still to her ear, her spare hand covering the mouthpiece.

"Hi!" I whisper, grinning at her, as if I know her really well, which, of course, I don't. Her eyes alight on the trio behind me, and narrow slightly. "Hello," she says, with something like a question in her voice.

"Louisa," Tony says. "Hi. I didn't realise you were in town."

"Yes. I've come to see my mum," she says, in what I can't say is the warmest of tones.

Once we've passed by, leaving her to her phone call, I fall back to Tony, letting the others walk on ahead.

"You know Louisa?"

"Yes, our companies have been working together for a while."

165

"Well, she's Elise's daughter!"

"Elise?"

"Yes, my friend I've told you about! Who you just met in the restaurant!"

"Oh… right. That Elise. Sorry."

"How many Elises do you know?" I ask.

"Not many!" he laughs. "Sorry. It was just weird seeing somebody from work out of context."

"Oh yeah, I know what you mean. It's like seeing somebody who normally serves you in a shop, or a restaurant, but at the swimming pool or something." I'm slightly tipsy, I realise, and slurring my words slightly.

"What a great analogy," he grins, cheekily.

"Watch it," I say, and I take his hand, then place my other hand on his arm. The rest of the group have got slightly further ahead, and I take my chance to turn Tony towards me for a swift kiss.

"Hello," he smiles.

"Hi."

We look at each other for a moment, and then walk hand-in-hand down the hill, catching up with the rest of my family, then heading onto the busy beach. We are not dressed for it, but we take off our shoes – the men removing socks as well, and rolling up their trouser legs – and walk barefoot along the shore, dodging children and adults who shriek and splash in the water. The six of us walk to the far end, where we clamber onto the rocks – Tony helping my mum, I note with a smile – and just stop for a while, soaking up the sun, and watching the gentle waves rolling in towards us.

# 2007

Planning the wedding was the stuff of Julia's dreams. Maggie knew her sister had very set ideas about how the day should go: what she wanted to wear; what she wanted Paul to wear; the colour scheme; the cake. These kinds of things had never even crossed Maggie's mind, so it was an eye-opener to her, to realise just how much planning and detail were necessary for the one 'big day'.

She had to admit, though, it was fun. In the months leading up to the wedding, she was in Cornwall a number of times, and Julia and Lucy came up to Bristol to go wedding dress shopping, which was a lovely day. They stayed the night, Lucy in the spare room of Maggie's flat, and Julia sharing Maggie's bed. They went out to eat Mexican food and drink cocktails, walking, giggling, back up Zetland Road.

"I miss Bristol sometimes," Lucy admitted.

"Do you, Mum?"

"Well, yeah, of course. I mean, I wouldn't move back here. I don't know if I could now. I just don't think I'm cut out for city living any more. Too much traffic, for one thing. But of all the cities, Bristol has to be the best. Maybe I'll win the lottery and get a little flat up here so I can come for weekends."

"What's wrong with my flat?" Maggie had laughed.

"Nothing! Obviously. But you won't want your old mum hanging round every weekend. I'd cramp your style."

"True."

Crossing Redland Green, the three figures passed under the intermittent streetlamps, arms linked, and ever-so-slightly unsteady on their feet. To an onlooker, they might have been three friends on a night out, and, essentially, they were, Maggie thought. Maybe it was the cocktails, but she'd never felt so grateful for the relationship she had with her mum and sister.

When they left the next day, taking the train out of Temple Meads, Maggie decided she would walk all the way home, giving her time and space to think about her own life. Yes, her sister was young to get married, by modern standards, but she was the same age Lucy had been when she'd married Jeff.

As Maggie walked the long, exhaust-darkened pavements, past the busy roads of the city centre, she thought of her failed relationship with Andy (if it could even be called a relationship), which she knew had been a non-starter. Then Adrian, who she knew had really liked her, but she hadn't felt the same. Now that her old housemate Mali was living with her boyfriend Leon, and Angela had just announced that she and partner Jodie were set to find a place together, Maggie was feeling it. Eventually, her mind turned to Stacey, and her various efforts to usurp Maggie, or at least that was how it had seemed at the time. From first year to fifth year, it had seemed that whoever Maggie liked, they always liked Stacey, or Julia. It was never Maggie. And yes, she was happy in her work, and her flat, and she could do what she liked, when she liked, but if she was very honest, that didn't really amount to much. An expensive, rarely-used gym membership attested to this, and a lot of lazy weekends, with fewer and fewer nights out as, all around her, friends seemed to be pairing off and settling down.

Crisis-point was too strong a term for what she was going through, but it did seem fairly pivotal, that her very own twin sister was about to tie herself to somebody for life while she, Maggie, had not so much as a date on the horizon.

As she walked up past the Royal Infirmary, panting slightly, she felt like she had an epiphany. She needed to make some changes. Inside that building were people who were dying, or ill, or about to find out they were ill. There were of course people who were recovering, too, and people about to find out they were recovering, or were not going to die (not yet, at least). Either way, though, there were people in there going through the mill, and there was she on the outside. Mid (late) twenties, puffing her way up this hill, an unused gym membership and hours of free time at her disposal. The first thing she had to do was obvious. Get fit. Not for anyone else. Not to be more attractive (well, OK, maybe a little bit of that), but for herself. A healthy body equals a healthy mind, she told herself. And when she got back to her flat, she dug out her gym kit, and her dog-eared membership card, and was down at the gym within the hour.

Red-faced as she strode out on the treadmill, she thought of how Lucy and Julia would nearly be back home by now. Paul would no doubt be waiting to pick them up at the station. It was just second nature to Julia by now, her relationship, and Maggie wondered how it would feel to be so comfortable with somebody – to even take them for granted.

Julia had looked so beautiful in her dress. Maggie had been quite surprised by the sharp tears which pricked her eyes at the sight of her sister in a beautiful ivory gown. She had known Lucy would cry, of course, but she hadn't expected to feel that way herself. And she was excited about being bridesmaid, even if James Watson was best man, and there would no doubt be the usual jokes about the best man and bridesmaid. Ha, ha, ha. It was annoying, though, that there were James and Adrian, who were both so lovely and decent, who had seemed to like her, but for whom she felt little but friendship. Affection, at the most.

She pounded out some more steps, increasing the speed a little to try and expel some of her frustration. There was a room-long mirror on the wall in front of the machines, and she could see herself as others might see her. Sort of ordinary, really. Not fat, not thin. Not ugly, not beautiful. No wonder nobody was interested in her.

In the four months leading up to Julia's wedding, Maggie went to the gym five days out of seven, every week. She usually walked to work, then went to the gym after she had left the office, which was one way to shorten those otherwise long, empty evenings. On Sundays, she'd spend a good couple of hours there, finishing off with a leisurely swim, and a sauna. She began to see how it could be quite addictive, but whether or not she'd continue after the wedding, she wasn't sure. Perhaps it was a premature mid-life crisis. Or really, she just wanted to be at her best at the wedding, so that nobody would pity her for being on her own. She was also aware that Stacey Pattern was going to be there, with her boyfriend. Maggie would play it cool with her, she decided, but would be civil. And she was determined to look her absolute best, to show just how far she had come.

These days, nights out were now more often evenings in, at friends' houses, as it began to dawn on them that they needed to hold on to some of their hard-earned money, for mortgages, cars, holidays, and even, eventually, families. There was a wave of realisation rolling over the heads of her group of friends, and they broke the surface, eyes stinging but seeing clearly that life could not go on forever with them spending every available (and sometimes unavailable) penny on clothes and CDs, booze and nightclubs. Maggie also felt like some of her group were enjoying playing house, moving in with partners, cooking, cleaning, organising shared social lives; becoming, in Maggie's view, exactly the kind of women they had vowed they never would, but now apparently relishing the role of home-maker, without relinquishing their careers. Was it having it all, or was it making a rod for your own back, and running yourself into the ground? This was yet to become apparent.

Maggie had booked her two weeks in Cornwall so that Julia's wedding fell squarely in the middle. She had a feeling that she would need the second week for a break, as the first promised to be fairly full-on. There was a lot to this wedding-planning malarkey, at least when it was her sister making the plans.

She took the train down and was collected from the station by Paul and a very excited, but slightly stressed, Julia.

"Hi, sister," said Paul, smiling as she clambered into the back seat, Julia climbing in next to her.

"Brother Paul," Maggie said. "Sorry, you must feel like a chauffeur with us both in the back."

"It's no bother."

"Home, James!"

"Speaking of James…" Julia said.

"What about him?"

"He's just split up with his girlfriend."

"Oh, right, I didn't even know he had a girlfriend."

"Yes, well, I thought I'd mention it. Just in case…"

"Julia," Paul said warningly. "You said you wouldn't say anything."

"Yes, well, I know, but I can't help it, can I? I'm – *we're* – so in love. And so lucky. And so happy—"

Maggie opened her car door window and pretended to be sick out of it.

"Maggie!" laughed Julia good-naturedly. "I'm just saying. You know he's had a thing about you forever."

"I know no such thing. And besides, you and Paul are love's young dream. There can't be room for more than one long-term relationship from our school year. I'll be pleased to see James again, of course, he's a lovely bloke, but don't go match-making. Please."

"OK."

"I mean it."

"Fine."

Paul met Maggie's eye via the mirror, and she saw he was smiling. Her sister was a lucky woman, for sure. But Maggie knew she had to find her own way in the wider world. It would be harder than Julia's path, perhaps, but it would be worth it in the end.

# Maggie

The week with Julia, Paul and Mum goes by so quickly. Work has suddenly stepped up a gear, and I'm out meeting local groups, and small businesses, and charities, most mornings. I'm torn between wanting to see Tony, and wanting to see my sister, but luckily Tony sees this and insists I make the most of my family being nearby.

"I'm not going away anytime soon," he says, kissing me. "And anyway, you can always stop by my place on your way home."

With Stevie staying at Mum's again this week, I have taken him up on his offer, and stayed over every night so far. I've gone over to Mum's every evening, and we've had a barbecue on the beach two nights, the weather has been so utterly perfect. Although I've been at work all week, having Julia and Paul and Mum on holiday here, paired with the blue skies and endless sunshine, has lent me a kind of holiday feeling as well, so that I've been staying up late every night, and really not minding the lack of sleep. The nights are becoming dark far earlier now, though, reminding me that autumn is not far away.

Out at Tony's, the sky is so clear, with minimal light pollution to fade out the stars. We've sat on the chairs outside his back door, well into the early hours of the morning, just chatting, or even saying nothing, sipping glasses of wine, holding hands, and letting the summer cradle us in its warmth. But now it's Friday, and tomorrow Julia and Paul go home – and on Tuesday Mum will do the same. I have taken Wednesday to Friday as annual leave, and then it's bank holiday Monday, and then – which I can still barely believe – on Wednesday, Stevie starts secondary school. I was going to take the Tuesday off work, too, but she's been invited to her friend Josie's house, which I found disappointing somehow. I don't know what I imagined – a kind of solemn last day of childhood – because there is no getting around the fact that when you go to secondary school, things change. I'd hoped to spend this last day of innocence with her, but it seems I would be redundant, so I might as well save my leave for half-term. Maybe we'll go up to Mum's then. Or perhaps Stevie will be exhausted, and just need some downtime. God, I wouldn't go back to the start of secondary school if you paid me. The timetables. The teachers, the corridors, the older kids... I suppose because Julia and I were the new kids in town, it was even more scary. We didn't know anyone, aside from having been introduced to Stacey by our parents. We had each other, and we tried to welcome Stacey in, as if she needed looking after. She was more than capable of looking after herself. I can see that first day at secondary now as if it were yesterday. I remember the feeling, as Julia and I walked up that path towards the school, which loomed in front of us, its two huge doors open, like a mouth that would close and swallow us, or spit us out, as it chose. Nervously making our way

174

between groups of happy, chattering children; I wanted to hold Julia's hand, but of course that would have been tantamount to a death wish, and Julia would certainly not have thanked me for it. Her extra inch of height seemed more like a foot that day – she held her head high, as befitted her dancer status, and I felt so small and bowed in comparison. We were ushered into a room with a couple of other kids who had moved into the area – who to my shame I don't remember now. My head was turned by Stacey, as I suspect was true for us all. She ruled the roost – addressing Mr Hayward, the history teacher, almost as though he were an equal. It came from being an only child, my mum said – and spending most of her time with adults. As we had requested to be in different forms, Julia and I, it was my hope that I'd be with Stacey, but of course she was put with Julia, and I remember seeing them walk off, guided by a third-year boy, all chatting and laughing as they went. Mr Hayward took me to my form room. I had glanced once more at my sister and our new friend, seeing them disappear around the corner of a corridor, and I felt so alone. My stomach felt as though somebody was wringing it out. I honestly don't know if that sensation has ever entirely gone away since.

But that is a long time ago now, and I am sure that Stevie's experience of school will be so different to mine. I always thought she would be just like me, but she is way more confident, and sure of herself and her place in the world. She already knows all about toxic friendships, and has no time for attention-seekers. She is friends with the girls, but she also likes to hang out with boys; I suspect because they seem less complicated at this age. I push my own memories away, and look forward to the evening ahead. We are going for a pizza at the restaurant by the harbour, at Stevie's request, and then we're going to head back up to Mum's flat for a few games of cards, and a drink or two, and Stevie and I are both staying over. I will miss seeing Tony, but I've begun to accept that he is, as he says, not going anywhere anytime soon.

# 2007

The wedding day dawned as all wedding days should – bright and sunny, with barely a cloud in the sky. Maggie had slept in Julia's room, on the single mattress they had used when a schoolfriend – usually Stacey – had stayed over. It had felt quite fun, having a sleepover, and also quite momentous. Even though Julia was by now living with Paul, this final night for her as a Cavendish had seemed poignant. The girls had shared a takeaway curry with Jeff and Lucy, although it was only Maggie who seemed to have any appetite.

"You don't look like there's room for all that food!" Jeff had said, as she piled another poppadom with onion and mango chutney.

"Jeff!" Lucy had exclaimed. "You don't make remarks like that. But you have lost some weight, love," she added. "You looked lovely before, though. You didn't need to lose anything."

"But I'm so much stronger now!" Maggie had flexed her muscles, making them all laugh. She was, though, proud of herself, for the hours she'd put in at the gym. It wasn't something she really enjoyed, but it had been a challenge, and every time she'd seen herself in that mirror opposite the treadmills, she thought she looked better, and far less red-faced these days. It was nice to be fit, but she had already decided to pack in the gym. She would exchange it for walking to and from work, she had decided. That thirty-minute walk twice each day, up and down to the centre, was good exercise. The idea of running had also crossed her mind, but she was pretty sure it would stay an idea – for now.

Still, she had set her mind to getting fit, and to looking at her absolute best at her sister's wedding, and she had achieved both these aims. It was something to be proud of.

"You do look good, Maggie," Julia said thoughtfully. She still had her dancer's physique, and Maggie couldn't imagine that would ever change. Even if she had twelve babies, Julia would surely be as slim and willowy and flexible as ever.

"Thanks, sis. You look OK, too!"

Their parents had laughed at this exchange, pleased that their girls still got on so well. But then Jeff had become a little bit tearful, taking them all by surprise.

"I knew this day would come," he sniffed, "when you'd both be grown up and gone. And I want you to know how proud I am of you. And I may not have been the best dad, or husband—"

"Jeff," Lucy had interjected with a slight note of warning in her voice. Maggie looked at Julia to see if she'd picked up on it, but her twin was just looking shiny-eyed, no doubt caught up in the romance of the situation.

"No, I mean it, Lucy. I haven't been the best. But I've tried to make up for it. And I've never stopped loving you. Any of you."

"We know, Dad," Maggie put her hand on his, touched by his outburst, but also slightly concerned. "And you have been the best. You are the best!"

"Yes!" Julia echoed. "Of course you are, Dad. And you know I've been living with Paul for ages now, and Maggie buggered off to Bristol years before that."

"I did not bugger off to Bristol!" Maggie protested.

"Of course you did! But that's fine. You're happy there. You are, aren't you?"

Now Julia was in tears. What was going on? Only Maggie and Lucy had dry eyes now. She looked at her mum, who may not have been crying, but also looked a bit sad.

"This is meant to be a happy occasion!" Maggie exclaimed. "Julia's getting married tomorrow. You'll have a beautiful day – you'd better, after all the work you've put into it. Dad, nothing will change at all, except maybe you'll have some grandchildren to play with sometime soon. And Mum, well, OK, you haven't actually said anything, but can we all please just cheer up and enjoy this? It's a wedding, not a funeral!"

This had made them all laugh, as Maggie had hoped it would, and Jeff had taken the hint, physically pulling himself up straight, and vowing to stop making such a sentimental fool of himself.

So Maggie had woken up on the single mattress, on the floor of her sister's childhood bedroom. The thin curtains immediately gave away what kind of weather was awaiting them, and the sound of a blackbird singing in the tree just outside Julia's bedroom window lifted Maggie's heart.

"Julia!" she hissed. Somehow, even though it was her wedding day, Julia was blissfully asleep.

"Wha–" she screwed her eyes up, as though trying her best to stay in that sleep, then they sprang open. "Oh my god! I'm getting married!"

"You are!" Maggie laughed. "You're getting bloody married! To Paul bloody Cooper!" She clambered onto Julia's bed and hugged her sister, pulling back the curtains to reveal what had already been promised. "And what a day for it!"

"Oh my god, oh my god, oh my god!" Julia's nerves went into overdrive, and Maggie knew she'd have to try and keep a lid on them over the course of the morning. This was the problem with an afternoon wedding, she thought. There were an awful lot of hours to fill before the event.

But fill them they did, and more quickly than Maggie had imagined they might. The day began with a breakfast in the garden. Maggie, Julia and Lucy still in their pyjamas. Jeff was up and dressed, and preparing pancakes and fresh berries, with a huge cafetiere of hot coffee, a jug of cream, and freshly-squeezed orange juice.

They sat at the table at the end of the garden, surrounded by evergreens and apple trees, which were buzzing with bees. Birdsong and a soft perfumed sweetness filled the air. The grass was already yellowing in spots, from the hot, dry weeks that had stretched from spring into summer.

"I wish Pretzel was here," Maggie said.

"Me too," said Julia.

"He was a good dog," Jeff said. He raised his glass of juice. "To Pretzel."

"To Pretzel," they all agreed, raising glasses and mugs.

There was a general air of nervous excitement, but also a general sense of reluctance to break up this meal. Maggie realised she understood what Jeff had meant the previous night. From now on, there may be no more meals for the four of them. Paul would very likely be with Julia – but surely not all the time, would he? They might be getting married, but they weren't being surgically attached to each other. Did it mean things would change, though? She supposed it must. And maybe Julia and Paul wanted to have children soon. She didn't know, she hadn't asked. Maybe this time next year there would be a baby in a bassinet, or whatever they were called, alongside them. Perhaps this really was it, and last night the Last Supper. Still, it was normal, and natural, and she just knew that they would remain as close as ever, whatever changes came their way. But maybe it was a good idea to sit back and take it in, this golden morning of sunshine and family togetherness. And she did. She sat back for a few moments, watching Julia stir some cream into her coffee, and Lucy mop up the juice from the berries with a last scrap of pancake. When Maggie looked at Jeff, she saw he was doing the same as her. He smiled at her, and understood.

In time, Lucy stood up. "Come on," she said. "There's much to do before this afternoon. Girls, into the shower. You first, Julia. And remember, don't wash your hair! Marlene won't be able to get it to stay up as well if it's too clean."

"OK, Mum," Julia said, in a passable imitation of her usual teenage response to Lucy's commands. It made Lucy and Jeff laugh, and somehow made it easier to break up the little party.

"We'll clear up, won't we, Maggie?" Jeff asked.

"Of course."

So Lucy and Julia went into the house, leaving Maggie alone with her dad.

"It's weird, isn't it?" she asked.

"It is a bit… you could probably tell that I'm finding it a bit emotional. After my little speech last night. Sorry."

"It's fine! It was nice. But, just for the record, you were, and are, a great dad. OK?"

"OK." He smiled. "Thank you, love." And he pulled her into him, kissing her on the top of the head. "I'm proud of you, Maggie. You and your sister both. You're both doing your own thing, but I really admire you for being so bloody independent. You're going to go far, I know it. You'll have your own PA before too long!"

"I don't know about that," Maggie said, thinking that if she did have her own PA, she wouldn't expect her – or him – to get her coffee, or collect dry cleaning, or buy presents for her partner, as Michael her boss seemed to expect her to do for his wife, Janet.

"I don't know what I'd do without you," he'd say, no doubt thinking it a compliment, and utterly missing the look of disdain and disappointment on Maggie's face. It wasn't that he was a horrible man; he was very pleasant, and kind-hearted, too, but he seemed to expect to be waited on, and he took the term 'personal assistant' to the extreme. At least he'd never tried it on with her, though, as she knew some of her friends' managers had with them.

She shook her head free of work thoughts. "Thanks, Dad." She kissed him on the cheek. "We'd better get this lot inside and washed up now, before the day runs away with us."

"You sound just like your mum," he'd smiled. "And that is a very good thing. Go on, you carry them in, and

I'll wash up while you have your shower. I have a feeling your sister's going to need you this morning."

Maggie luxuriated in the heat of the shower, and the perfume of Lucy's expensive body wash, knowing that as soon as she stepped out of the cubicle and wrapped that towel around her, it would be all systems go.

Marlene had already arrived by the time Maggie was in her shorts and t-shirt; fancy bridesmaid underwear already on, and at odds with the plain, boyish clothes.

Julia was in her thin dressing gown, sitting at the dressing table in their parents' room. Her dress, and Maggie's and Lucy's, hung from the large wooden wardrobe, and the open windows let in the gentlest of breezes, and the sounds of some neighbours' children playing in their paddling pool; blissfully unaware of the significance of this date for the Cavendishes. Further away came the steady hum of a lawnmower, casting Maggie's mind back to summer nights when she'd lie in bed with the daylight still going strong outside, and their next-door neighbour mowing the lawn. There was something nice about going to sleep while life was still very much going on. It felt safe, and reassuring, and so different to the cold dark of winter, when at the very same time of night it might be windy and raining, and branches could cast shadows across the windows.

"Here," Lucy said, bringing in a tray of four glasses of champagne. "Your dad sent these up. He said not to bring the bottle so we don't drink too much! But there's more downstairs if we want it."

"Cheers." Marlene and the three Cavendish women clinked glasses together, but Maggie noticed Marlene didn't touch her drink, until she'd finished Julia's, then Lucy's, and finally Maggie's, hair. By this time, Maggie, Julia and Lucy were already on their second glasses.

"I don't suppose you do make-up as well, do you, Marlene?" Maggie asked. "I just think that the mixture of champagne and nerves might mean we're not quite at our best!"

"Of course, my love. Leave it to me," Marlene said. She picked colours that Maggie would never have chosen for herself: soft pinks around her eyes, and on her cheekbones, and on her lips. Maggie never wore lipstick. She liked the result.

"You look gorgeous!" Julia exclaimed. "You'd better not go upstaging me."

"Unlikely," said Maggie, admiring her sister. With her hair pinned up and just a few curls cascading down, and some smoky dark eye make-up, she looked like a model. "Oh god," Maggie said. "I think I'm going to cry. You might have to redo my eye make-up, Marlene."

"No need," Marlene said proudly. "All waterproof, look. Perfect for weddings!"

In the corner of the room, Lucy was also shedding a quiet tear.

"Come here, Mum," Maggie said, and she pulled her mum and her sister towards her for a hug. "I love you two."

"I love *you* two," said Lucy.

"And *I* love you two," Julia added.

"It might be waterproof, but I don't know if it will stand up to all that, you know," Marlene laughed. "Now, it's none of my business really, but I do think you need to be getting dressed."

And so they did. They exclaimed over each other, and left the room to walk down the stairs and find Jeff. It was his turn for tears ("At least you're not wearing mascara, Dad!") and then another very small glass of champagne each to toast each other. Marlene left, with the flowers that Julia had bought for her, an envelope of cash, and a bottle of champagne of her own. And then the car arrived, adorned with cream ribbons, and the Cavendish family walked out of their house, locking the door behind them.

# Maggie

There is a light drizzle as we walk down to the harbour, but we don't care. Stevie walks between me and Mum, and we see Paul and Julia leaning on the harbour railings, watching the boats. Before they realise we're approaching, Paul puts his arm around Julia, and pulls her in for a kiss and a hug. They look happy.

"Enough of that, you two!" I say, though, pretending to barge in between them.

"Hey!" Julia laughs. "Watch it!"

"Or what?"

"You know I can take you down," she says.

"There'll be none of that, thank you," Paul says, putting an arm round each of us. "Now, are you going to escort me to this fine restaurant young Stephanie has recommended?"

"Don't call me that!" Stevie exclaims.

"Why not? It's your name, isn't it? And I believe that once you're all grown up at secondary school, you must be called by your full name. Isn't that right, Maggie?"

"Yes, exactly. It's Stephanie from now on. Sorry, Stevie... I mean Stephanie."

"Well why do you get called Maggie, then, and not Margaret?" she says triumphantly.

"You've got me there."

"Hey! Julia! Maggie!" we hear from behind us, just as

we're about to walk through the restaurant door. Mum, Paul and Stevie have already gone in.

We all turn, and my heart almost stops.

"Stacey!" Julia says. "What are you doing here?"

"Well, when you were talking about it last week," Stacey says, air-kissing each of us in turn, "I thought, we live in Cornwall, but we've never been all the way down here, and I've heard so much about it. So we booked a last-minute thing for the bank holiday! Isn't it great?"

She is dressed in a pair of white linen trousers and a stripey top, looking trim and petite and as though there is no way she could possibly have been pregnant once, never mind three times. A pair of oversized sunglasses nest in her hair. She looks, undeniably, gorgeous, and glamorous. But I no longer feel that sense of envy I used to have. Instead, this time, it is panic. She said 'we'. Which can only mean one thing. Sure enough, wandering out of the ice-cream shop next door, each clutching a waffle cone in their hands, come Sean, and three tall, tanned, and lovely-looking boys.

Sean stops, and the tallest of the boys bumps into him.

"Dad!" He exclaims. He is a similar age to Stevie, I'd guess.

"Hi Sean!" says Julia. "You remember my sister, Maggie?"

"Yeah, of course. Hi, Maggie. How are you?"

"I'm fine, thanks. How are you? And you, Stacey? I can't believe you're here! We're just about to go for pizza…"

"Do you want to join us?" Julia says.

*Please say no. Please say no.*

"Oh, no thanks, we've just been to that new place," says Stacey. "You know, the one with the Michelin star, and the waiting list a year long? Sean managed to pull a few strings."

*I bet he did.* I am relieved, though.

"Ah well, we'd better go in," I say.

"Yes, I'll see you back home, no doubt," Julia says to Stacey. "Paul and I are going back tomorrow. But you should give Maggie a shout over the weekend…"

"Oh, I think I'll be busy, getting Stevie set for school," I say hurriedly.

"And seeing *Tony*," Julia laughs.

My cheeks are so red, and I hate myself for it.

Sean looks at me, like he's holding in a laugh.

"Oh, who's Tony?" Stacey asks.

"Just… my boyfriend." My god, why do I feel like I'm about fourteen again?

"Maybe we should go on a double date!" she exclaims.

"That sounds lovely," I say, disingenuously. "But Stevie's starting secondary school next week, and we've got so much to do."

I surreptitiously look at Sean, wondering if the mention of secondary school will mean anything to him, but it looks to all intents and purposes as though it's gone over his head.

"Come on, Mum," the smallest of the three boys tugs at Stacey's hand. "You said we could go to the arcade."

"I did." She looks at me, and Julia and rolls her eyes. "Honestly, who'd have thought there'd be an amusement arcade here? I thought this was an upmarket place."

"Don't be such a snob!" Sean smiles at me as he says it, as though we're the best of friends. "Come on, boys. Nice to see you again, Maggie. Bye, Julia." He turns, and the boys troop after him, pleased to have left their parents' boring friends behind. I can't help watching them, and smiling at the way they jostle each other.

With another air kiss, Stacey is on her way, with her beautiful, well-dressed family. "We must catch up properly soon," she says to me.

"We really must." I smile. Like hell we must.

# 2007

The service was beautiful; the church bedecked with orange, gold, yellow and cream flowers, with small bunches fastened to the ends of the pews, and larger displays on either side of the altar.

Lucy had gone in already, and Maggie's stomach was tying itself in knots as she heard the organ strike the opening chords of the Wedding March, and saw Jeff give Julia a little hug and a kiss, turning briefly to smile encouragingly at Maggie before they began the walk in through the doors, and up the aisle.

All eyes were on Julia, of course, and Maggie knew that, but she couldn't help feeling like she stood out a little, walking alone behind her twin and her dad. Were people wondering where her partner was? Or for those in the know, wondering why she didn't have one. Or, worst of all, was the fact she didn't have a partner something to be expected? She just hoped nobody pitied her. The spinster sister.

She gave herself a mental kick. This was a fruitless train of thought. *Futile*, she said to herself, remembering Mark Beaumont's rejection of Stacey. She, Maggie, was young, and had plenty of time to find somebody. And besides, this day was not about her in any shape or form.

As they approached the altar, she saw Paul looking at Julia, and his expression made her catch her breath. That was love, right there. And she looked at Julia, to see she was shaking a little. Paul clearly saw it, too, and as Jeff stepped back to take his place next to Lucy, Paul took Julia's hand and they stood together in front of the vicar. Maggie stepped to Julia's left side, while James stood to Paul's right. This was as they had practised in the rehearsal the previous afternoon. James had greeted her with a peck on the cheek, and it had been good to see him. He seemed hardly to have changed across the years, and was as kind and friendly as ever. She wondered now whether he still had a crush on her, and whether she could feel differently about him – but no. There was nothing there but friendship, on her part at least. Hopefully these days it was the same for him. What was his ex-girlfriend like? She pictured somebody lovely and wholesome and sensible. But she didn't know James these days, and maybe he had changed over the years.

She pulled her thoughts back to the situation before her. Her sister getting married. She watched Julia, and listened to the words of the vicar, and her sister, and her nearly-brother-in-law. She could not see Julia's face, but she could see Paul's, and it said all she needed to know. The rings were exchanged, and then there was the first kiss as husband and wife, and a spontaneous round of applause resounded around the cool stone walls of the church. Then there was a slightly less romantic legal element, when Julia and Paul signed the required documentation, and then the service was over – Maggie and James walking arm-in-arm behind the happy couple. Maggie felt Julia's relief, that the nerve-racking part of the day was done, and now it was out into the warmth of the sun, and time for the celebrations to begin.

Maggie glanced along the aisle as she walked, seeing relatives, and friends of old – and some of Julia's work friends, who she didn't know – on one side, while Paul's family and friends occupied the other. She noticed a fluttering to her right and saw Stacey waving at her, smiling widely. She looked gorgeous, of course, with a cream jacket over a low-cut navy dress, and a cream fascinator in her hair. Maggie smiled at Stacey, and glanced swiftly at the man next to her, who was tall and good-looking, with a skater-style haircut, cropped close to his scalp all over, matching the length of his stubble. He was also wearing a cream suit, with a light blue shirt, open at the neck. Most of the other men were in work suits, of navy or grey, so this man – presumably Sean, Stacey's boyfriend from Leeds – stood out. As she took all this in, she also realised he was looking at her, and he offered her a smile, which sent her own gaze scurrying away, back to the rear of her sister's head, and Julia's beautiful dancer's shoulders, bare and lightly tanned, with not a strap line in sight. Maggie knew how much thought had gone into achieving that effect, and she wished she'd had the forethought, feeling grateful for the small, short-sleeved shrug she had to cover her own freckled, tan-marked shoulders, which bore the clear tan lines from vest straps.

James squeezed her arm as they walked through the door and into the sunshine, then let go of her. "It's really good to see you again," he said. "And in the most platonic way, can I ask for the first dance with you? It's going to be expected of us anyway."

"Of course," she smiled, and put her hand on his arm. "That would be lovely." She was glad he'd got in there first with the platonic line, and would be glad to have him as back-up and company when, almost inevitably, the couples would pair off and she would otherwise be left alone. Thank god James had split up with his girlfriend, she thought, selfishly.

She kissed and hugged Julia, then Paul, then stood in line, next to James, with her parents and Paul's parents next to her, to greet the guests as they trailed outside. There was happy chatter and laughter everywhere, and Maggie realised how pleased she was to see her cousins, and her aunts and uncles, come together from various parts of the country.

When Stacey emerged, she was clutching Sean's hand, and Maggie saw her exclaiming to Julia, how beautiful she looked, and how lovely the service had been, and how amazing it was that Julia had married Paul, how much she missed those school days, etc.

"Maggie, I hardly recognised you. You look so… slim, and pretty." Stacey was now in front of her, and while this remark might easily be taken as a compliment, Maggie was well aware of the undertones. She'd been hearing them since she was eleven. *"I wish that I wasn't bothered about putting on weight, like you." "I like the way you don't care what people think about your appearance, Maggie." "You've got your own style, haven't you, Maggie? Not like me and Julia. I wish I wasn't so bothered about having to have fashionable clothes."*

Every time, the remarks were double-edged. On the face of it, a compliment. Maggie offered a smile and a thank you now, and accepted Stacey's hug. She always felt such a giant next to her – even now, with her new, improved body, she couldn't change her height.

Sean offered his hand to shake, and as their eyes met,

he smiled at Maggie. And what a smile. Maybe he knew it was a gorgeous smile – almost certainly he would have been told so more than once – but he seemed genuine enough. As he and Stacey moved along, and Maggie continued to greet the line of guests, she thought about her old friend, and the antipathy she now felt towards her. Julia presumably saw Stacey differently, but then Julia had always been on a par with her, in terms of popularity, and looks. Maggie had been, or at least felt, a poor second, and Stacey had done nothing to disabuse her of that notion.

Now, though, Maggie was aware of something else. Sean looking at her, with interest. Which was completely wrong, of course. He was Stacey's boyfriend, and that was the only reason he was here. Still, she found herself returning his gaze, surprised by her own boldness. Half hoping Stacey would notice, half terrified of the same thing. Stacey had never been one to avoid conflict, while Maggie would try to at all costs.

As the majority of people moved away, it was time for photos, with parents and friends and cousins, and then just the bridal party, and finally the happy couple. And then they emerged through the archway of the churchyard, into a cloud of fluttering rose petals, which scattered on the breeze back past them, skimming the pavement and grass, and catching on gravestones.

Paul and Julia were in the wedding car, and Lucy, Jeff and Maggie split between relatives for lifts to the reception. At the hotel, there were glasses of champagne, and more photos, while the guests tucked into canapes, and Maggie felt her stomach rumbling.

Then there was the dinner, and speeches, all of which made most people cry – but none more than Jeff's. James made everyone laugh, and told stories of their school days, then complimented Julia, and also Maggie, on how beautiful they looked. It made Maggie wish she had the nerve to stand up and speak on her twin's behalf, but she knew it would have been the only thing she'd have thought about all day, and the nerves would have got the better of her, so she was pleased for the good, old-fashioned sexism of wedding traditions and she could sit back and sip her cold champagne, with no more worries or responsibilities.

As promised, she danced the first dance (*The Luckiest*, by Ben Folds) with James, once Julia and Paul had been on the dancefloor alone for a minute or so, and she smiled at her old friend, realising how comfortable she felt, with somebody who had known her so long. Nearby, she was aware of Jeff dancing with Lucy, holding her close to him. They were happy, she knew, and this must be one of those stand-out days for parents, seeing your child married, happily. Would she have the chance to make them happy this way too, she wondered. Or would they have to be proud of her academic and career achievements? She remembered how Stacey used to say at school, "Maggie's the clever one." Another line that was actually more about what wasn't being said: Maggie was just clever – whereas Julia and Stacey were fun and talented, pretty and popular.

She had to leave all those school playground feelings behind, she knew. It was years ago now, and irrelevant, but somehow, seeing Stacey again, the insecurities and hurts she had suffered then, which had burrowed in deep, had found their way back to the surface, and it felt like leaving them behind was something far more easily said than done.

Still, as she and James moved past Stacey and her boyfriend, Maggie felt Sean's eyes on her again. She flicked a glance at him, confirming that he was indeed watching her, and she saw a small smile on his lips. It made her feel... what? Attractive, for one thing. And she couldn't deny that she felt pleased, that it was Stacey's boyfriend looking at her that way. She would never act on it, of course, even if he tried anything, which realistically was not going to happen, and she knew she wouldn't mention it to anyone. But it made her feel powerful, too. And she knew now, she wasn't 'just' clever, and she no longer needed Stacey's approval, or anyone else's. It hit her like a wave breaking over her: releasing all those old feelings, and washing them away.

She was young and free, and successful, and she had a wonderful family, and fantastic friends. Her future was a huge unknown, but wasn't everyone's? It felt suddenly exciting, rather than scary.

She laughed, and James looked at her. "Are you laughing at me?"

"No!" she said, hugging him, and kissing him on the cheek. "I'm just really, really happy."

# Maggie

"You're shaking," Julia says to me. "Are you alright?"

"Oh, yeah, I'm just really hungry. I didn't eat lunch today. It's probably low blood sugar, I guess."

"You really don't like Stacey, do you?" she asks.

"Why do you say that?"

"Well, you always manage to avoid her when you come back home."

Perhaps I haven't been as subtle as I've thought.

"I don't…"

"It's fine!" she squeezes my arm, leading me towards the table where the other three are waiting for us. "I know she wasn't very good to you at secondary school. I didn't really appreciate it then, and I'm sorry. But she's not so bad now, you know. And she's really settled down since she's become a mum."

"I'll take your word for it."

"I knew you didn't like her!" she laughs. "Now come on, let's order, I'm starving, too."

"Was that Stacey outside?" Mum asks, when we sit down. Paul and Stevie are engaged in a game of hangman.

"Yeah," I say. "Can you believe it?" Julia's right. I am shaking a little. I hold my hands together to steady them.

"You didn't invite her to join us, did you?" Mum laughs.

"No. You see, Maggie? You're not the only one who doesn't like her."

"Can't say I'm that fussed, either." Paul grins at me.

"And what about Sean?" I venture.

"You don't think he deigns to talk to me, do you? He's a big hotshot businessman. Not interested in a little family man like me."

"Paul," Julia says. "They're alright. And the boys are nice."

"If you like over-privileged, snotty-nosed children, sure."

I can't help laughing now. Stevie's ears have pricked up, too. "Who are you talking about?"

"Oh, just an old school friend and her family," I say.

"With three boys?"

"Yeah," I say. "Can you imagine?"

"I think she just reminds me too much of Sarah," says Mum.

I take a sneaky look at her. I haven't heard her mention that name in a while. "Have you seen Sarah recently?" I ask.

"Oh no, not since... well, not since your dad's funeral, I don't suppose." There doesn't seem to be any hidden emotion there. I don't press her any further.

"Anyway, are we going to eat, or what?" says Paul.

# 2009

The hours before the funeral went by in a blur, and felt like a sad, alternative version of the day that Julia and Paul had got married. Both days were sunny, and just as hot as each other.

Little had she expected to be back home on a similar day two years later, with her mum and her sister again, but this time with no Jeff downstairs, nervously checking his watch, eager to see the three women he loved so much, and happy to hear their laughter and chatter upstairs. He could have felt left out, but he just felt incredibly lucky.

There was no champagne, and no dressing to impress. All their dresses were simple designs, but none were black: dark green for Maggie, dark red for Julia, and a floral, dark blue for Lucy.

They dressed separately, each in their own rooms, each lost in their own thoughts, although they had enjoyed a relatively cheery breakfast together – more liquid (coffee and juice, not alcohol) than solid (croissants were left barely touched – the most Maggie could stomach was a yoghurt). This time, it was Paul waiting downstairs, sad at the loss of his father-in-law, and pale from worry about his wife and what this sudden loss of her dad might do to her. Julia had been distraught, inconsolable, and had only wanted her mum, and her twin. He had stood back, aware that there was nothing he could do, and fearful that she would shrug away any effort of consolation on his part.

"The car's here!" he called softly. He had been a part of this family for more than a few years now, and had of course known Julia and Maggie since they'd started school, but their closeness was almost unnerving today, and he felt like he couldn't break into it.

He didn't dare try.

There was no answer, so he called up again, a little louder this time, and he heard the sounds of footsteps soft on bedroom carpets, then three doors opening almost as one. And the trio of broken-hearted Cavendish women emerged, acknowledging each other, and squeezing hands.

As they came down the stairs, Paul reached for Julia, but she just shook her head and followed her mum. She could barely look at him. It was down to Maggie to smile at her brother-in-law, and put a hand lightly on his arm. "It's OK," she whispered.

Paul waited while they put on their shoes, then he opened the door for them, following them out and then waiting while Lucy locked it. He noticed the way she stopped for a moment, and imagined that she was considering the number of times she had done this before, with Jeff by her side. He dreaded this ever happening to him, and having to miss Julia so much. He thought briefly that he hoped he would die before her, then shook his head lightly, batting away the inappropriate thought.

In the long, black car, the four of them sat quietly; the three women on one seat together, holding hands, and Paul opposite them. He had no idea what to do, or what to say, but something told him he had no need to do or say anything. Just to be there. He felt better for knowing this. And, once they reached the woodland where the ceremony was being held, and he'd climbed out of the car, Julia took his hand and they walked together along the path, behind Maggie and Lucy. He felt part of things once more. Like he had a place.

Jeff had always said he wanted a humanist funeral. He'd expressed this wish many times, though he had not expected to need one so soon. It had been very sudden, his death. An embolism, in the toilets at work. It had been some time before anybody realised he was missing, because he usually worked alone in his office for much of the day.

His PA, Molly, began to wonder where he'd got to, and tried his mobile, then tried it again. It rang out both times. Something was not right. She knew it. But who to say this to? She walked the building alone first, looking for him on the shop floor, then the break room, and ringing his mobile sporadically. She heard his ringtone in the men's toilets and had to ask Dave Hawker, who she had a crush on, to go in and check on their boss. Dave found Jeff collapsed on the floor, near the sinks. He kept his cool, and turned Jeff over, checked for a pulse, listened for breath. It was no good, and Jeff's skin felt disturbingly cool.

Dave came back out to Molly, and told her what he'd found. She exclaimed, and turned pale, and Dave put his arms around her, then they called for an ambulance and tried to piece together what they had to do in a situation like this.

Dave and Molly had come to the funeral together, so Jeff's death had at least brought about one positive thing.

Jeff's wife and daughters and son-in-law approached the gathered mourners, who offered small smiles and light touches of arms, as the party walked by. The celebrant stood patiently and kindly, waiting, then greeted each woman in turn, then Paul as well.

Close by were Lucy's parents and brother Tim and his family, and Jeff's mum and dad. Behind them was Simon, Jeff's best friend from Bristol, and most of the other Bristol contingent, who had kept in touch over the years, and come for holidays, or at least called in, or met up for beach days if they were staying nearby. Then there were people from work, and neighbours and other friends from the town, and assorted people who the Cavendishes had 'collected' throughout their lives. Lucy's friends, and the twins'. Maggie had seen Claire and Ellie, who had remained good friends, Claire now living in Exeter, and Ellie in London. It was good of them to have come, she thought. And, of course, there was Stacey. She had brought Sean with her. And next to them was Sarah, with her second husband, Dylan. And was that Rob, next to them? Maggie hadn't seen Rob in a long time. It looked like he had brought somebody with him, too. A nice, understated-looking woman, who had her hand on Rob's arm.

Maggie's eyes had taken all this in, but her mind had taken longer to catch up, and now her thoughts had whirled around to the reason everybody was here. Her dad. Her dad was dead. He, or his body, was in that coffin. A carefully selected eco-friendly coffin, in fitting with his beliefs, and his funeral, and his committal in a green burial ground nearby. The woodland setting for the service was perfect, and peaceful, with birds singing unawares (or maybe they were fully aware, and singing especially for Jeff?) from the treetops, and in amongst the green, leafy branches. Out there, outside the trees, it was hot, but here it was cool and comfortable, and if the reason for them being there was not so terrible, Maggie would have loved it.

She and Lucy said a few words each about Jeff. Maggie had taken her time to write her speech, but in the end, she couldn't read it. Instead, looking at the coffin, she spoke from her heart: "Dad, you were a kind, funny and thoughtful man. You worked hard, but you never forgot about us, never let work become more important than your family. I loved–" she faltered – "spending time with you. Loved our family days at the beach–" here, she looked up at her mum and sister, who were watching her, and both smiled, and nodded – "and just, well, everything. You and Mum made our childhood happy, safe and secure. You were funny, and fun, and I never doubted how much you loved us all. I hope you knew, and still know, how much that love is returned and, though you've gone, the love never will." And she could say no more. Maggie looked at the celebrant, who was smiling kindly at her, then she walked back to her mum, falling against her side.

"That was beautiful, Maggie," Lucy whispered.

To close the service, Simon read a poem by James Fenton – about how the dead would want their loved ones to live on. Not to forget them, but to appreciate all that there is in life. Simon was in tears, and once he had finished, he came to Lucy's side, and she put her arm through his, and they walked together between the people gathered, back to the funeral car. Maggie and

Julia and Paul followed on, he in between the two sisters, holding a hand of each.

The car took them to the burial ground, where they were joined by close family only. Maggie sobbed as she saw her dad's coffin lowered into the hole, and they took it in turns to cast in some earth. Returning to the earth, she thought, and she knew it was right for her dad. She'd often wondered if she'd be freaked out by the thought of somebody she loved so much, buried in the ground. If she would be over-run by thoughts of what was going on down there, over time, but now she felt it was all ok. She had seen Jeff's body, at the undertakers. It had been horrendous. It had been OK.

She had been swept over by a feeling that he was alright, which was at odds with the fact that he was clearly dead, but – well, it was hard to explain – she had felt that, somehow, he was alright now. Still out there, somewhere. And still close by.

They all stood quietly for a while, then gradually each person turned and walked away. Maggie, Julia and Lucy were the last ones by the grave, with Paul standing back just a little, respectfully. He was strong and true and loyal, Maggie thought, and she was pleased that her sister had somebody so good in her life.

Maggie took one last look at the coffin, and turned her face up towards the blue sky. A lone seagull sailed silently by up above, and she thought that maybe, just maybe, it was him. Her dad. Come to see them all. And say his own goodbyes. Now, whenever she saw a lone gull, she couldn't help but think that it might be him. It brought her solace.

Afterwards, the mourners gathered at a beautiful, wood-built restaurant not far from the village. It was set amidst fields, and had a huge veranda, with a long wall of bifold doors, where people could sit and enjoy a cool drink and talk about Jeff – or anything else. Some of these people had not seen each other in years, and there was a lot to catch up on. They all agreed that they really must get together on a happier occasion and, though they meant it, they also knew it was unlikely to happen. Lives were already busy enough. However, many of them came back to Lucy and Jeff's house, at Lucy's invitation. She asked without thinking, aware that she wanted to prolong the end of this painful day, because surely then the real work of grieving began. Maggie had been looking forward to having the house to herself and her mum and her sister, and Paul, but she would do anything her mum wanted that day. So she and Julia and Lucy did the dutiful thing, and talked to everybody there, graciously accepting sympathies. It was exhausting. People wanted to engage her in conversation, and those she hadn't seen in years wanted to know about her life. Didn't they know it was inappropriate today, to talk about these things? The last thing she wanted was to discuss her job, or life in Bristol. Grateful for small mercies, at least she didn't have people asking her when she might be expecting her first child, as they seemed to think was an acceptable question for Julia, who had been married for a whole two years now so must surely be on the verge of motherhood.

Maggie felt she could sleep for a long, long time. But they were still here, the friends, and family, and work colleagues, of Jeff. Not all of them, of course. Her grandparents – Jeff's parents, and Lucy's mum and dad – had gone on to their hotel. They had judiciously and gratefully turned down Lucy's offer to stay with her: "You and the girls will want some space, love." Aunts and uncles had given hugs, shed tears, and made their sad way home. Now, it was mostly local people still gathered, most of whom were not family, and not necessarily great friends. Sarah and Rob had gone, with their respective partners, but not yet Stacey and Sean. Maggie wished they would. As the numbers dwindled, it would become harder to avoid Stacey. She wished that everyone would go now, in fact. What was the acceptable way to get rid of mourners, anyway? She stood on her own, leaning against the wall of the house, trying to count how many people were still there, and wondering how she might escape.

Then somebody brought out the whisky.

Paul and Julia did the sensible thing, and disappeared off to bed quite early. They had decided that, rather than go home, they would stay in Julia's childhood room – even though they only lived a few minutes' walk away. Lucy also had given in to sleep – or, more likely, tossing and turning, and trying to keep the excruciating pain of grief at bay. Still, the guests stayed on, and Maggie thought it must be her job to get rid of them, but she didn't know where to start, and didn't have the energy anyway.

Let them stay as long as they like, she thought. What difference would it make to anything? Still, she felt some antipathy towards them; chatting and drinking in her parents' garden, as though the world was still the same as ever, when she knew that it wasn't, and it never would be again.

It was a warm, still evening, and the remaining few were all outside, gathered in small groups in different parts of the garden. Maggie had just been inside to use the toilet and as she came out, she took a moment to take in the scene. She remembered Julia telling her she'd been given this advice on her wedding day – find a bit of time to take it all in, or else it would just go by in a whirl. Today, of course, was nothing like a wedding day, but Maggie still wanted to remember every detail. And maybe she wouldn't have a wedding day of her own, anyway. Maybe this was as close as she'd come to having all her family and friends gathered around her, for her. She was self-pitying, she knew, but it was how she felt sometimes. Everybody was pairing off, whereas it seemed she was now shedding people.

Stacey was chatting to James Watson, and some of the other old school gang, when Sean moved over to Maggie's side, sliding a glass into her hand. He raised his own glass. "To your dad."

"Did you know him?" Maggie asked, emboldened by the three glasses of whisky she had already drunk.

"No," he conceded. "But I feel like I did, after listening to your eulogy today. You were brilliant. If I'm ever a dad, I hope my kid talks about me the way you talked about him."

"Thank you." Maggie could feel herself blushing. She saw Stacey's head was turned towards them, and within moments, her former friend was there, putting a proprietary arm through Sean's.

"What are you two talking about, then?"

"Maggie's eulogy," Sean said.

Maggie loved the way 'eulogy' sounded in his northern accent.

"You were great," Stacey said. "I don't know if I could do that."

"You could, if you had to," Maggie said earnestly, touched by what seemed a genuine compliment, for once. "I know it doesn't feel like it, but when you're in this situation…"

"And you didn't mind saying all that, when, you know, your dad and my mum…?" Stacey interjected.

"Sorry… what?"

"You know, back when we were kids, when they…"

"Stace," Sean said, looking between his girlfriend and Maggie, and reading the situation.

"What? Oh," Stacey said. "You didn't know?" she asked Maggie.

"Know what?"

"Your dad, and my mum. They… Well, it didn't last long, but, and it was years ago, and…" Even Stacey, normally so obtuse, seemed to realise she was putting her foot in it here. Sean was jabbing her sharply in the ribs, while Maggie was just standing there, desperately trying to work out what she should do with her facial expression, and whether or not she could look like she knew all about this, while in fact it felt like the bottom had dropped out of her world.

"Sorry," Stacey rounded off with, sheepishly. "I thought you knew. I thought we all did. Julia does, doesn't she?"

"Does she? No, I don't think so," Maggie shook her

208

head vociferously. *She'd have told me if she knew... wouldn't she?*

"Well, your mum does, of course."

"Of course," Maggie agreed, hearing her voice emerging politely. She took a large swig from her glass. She felt Sean move closer to her side, and she realised it was just in time, as she felt faint. She rested herself against him. He felt firm and solid, like a tree. Rooted and strong, in this suddenly swaying world.

It had not even begun to feel real that her dad had died. That in itself was not possible. And now... now she discovered... what? Her dad had cheated on her mum? With *Sarah*? She couldn't see it somehow. Or could she? Did she remember Lucy sometimes making slightly sarcastic comments about Stacey's mum, and Jeff leaping to Sarah's defence? Would that have been before or after?

Stacey shuffled awkwardly. "Anyway, I was meant to be getting a drink for James over there—" she gestured towards their old friend – "so I'd better, you know..." she wheeled off and then walked more surely towards the kitchen door.

Sean stood there, dumbly, for a moment. "Erm..."

"It's fine. I knew all about it." Maggie heard the words coming from her mouth before she'd even thought them, or at least it felt that way.

"Did you?" Sean wasn't convinced, she could tell. She looked at him properly for the first time, and thought she saw a kindness in his eyes, which she hadn't noticed before.

"Do you want to... go for a walk, maybe?" she heard herself asking.

"Sure. Why not?"

"Why not?" She echoed, and laughed hoarsely. "Why the fuck not?"

Sean must have known she was vulnerable. There was no way that he couldn't have realised that. As the pair of them unlatched the garden gate and stepped out into the lane, Maggie brushed her fingers along the soft tops of the wild grasses and delicate flowers which grew along the verges and tumbled out of the rough-hewn stone walls of the gardens they passed by. Nothing felt real. It was like everything she did was being observed by some unseen, unknown audience. Like she was on a TV show, or in a play.

Soon enough, they were skirting past open countryside, on their way towards the sea, and something took it upon her to jump onto a stile, and into a field of sunflowers. And instead of sticking to the path around the edge of the flowers, she was running straight into the middle of them. It wasn't easy; they were sturdy and thick-stalked, and scratched at her bare skin, pulling at her clothes, but Maggie was determined.

Sean called her name, but she didn't reply, just kept pushing her way through the tall, hard stems, enjoying the slightly uncomfortable feeling on her bare arms.

She was surprised to hear him following behind her, and she laughed out loud. The sun was low in the sky, and would soon be disappearing behind the distant horizon, as far as the eye could see across the darkening sea. The night had a dusky, violet quality. Maggie thought of her little flat in Bristol, and the streets which were continuously rammed with parked cars, on either side. She loved the sunsets there, seeing the dashes of colour across the city skyline, and feeling that the place was still alive, no matter what the hour. Here, though, was peace. Tranquillity. A flock of small brown birds fluttered up out of the flowers, towards the patch of trees at the far reach of the field, their thin, reedy voices piercing tiny pinpricks in the silence.

The air was so still. Maggie put her hand on Sean's arm. She wanted him to feel it, too. It was like a spell. She looked at him, to see if he felt the same, and was shocked by her own sudden movement, her mouth finding his, and her breath seeming to stop for a moment, while her mind tried to catch up, to make sense.

Sean was warm, and strong, and solid. Real. Alive.

He returned her kiss, after just a moment's hesitation, and she tried not to think about Stacey. Tried to ignore that tiny, jubilant, childish 'Ha!' which she couldn't quite deny.

*This is for Robert Bastion.*

*This is for Mark Beaumont.*

*This is for every shitty, mean-minded little comment you've thrown my way.*

Then she lost herself in the kiss, aware that Sean's hands were moving now, stealthily, surely, around her waist, to the buttons on the front of her dress. Her body took over, giving her mind a break. She responded to his touch, as his fingers found their way under the soft cloth of the funeral dress. Warm.

Strong.

Solid.

*Alive.*

An image came, unbidden, of Jeff, with Sarah. Maggie screwed her eyes closed tighter.

"Are you OK?" Sean asked, breaking the train of thought, and she looked at him, laughed, and pulled him down into the field with her, the strong stalks bending and squashing under their weight.

An appropriately uncomfortable bed for a wholly inappropriate situation.

Afterwards, they laughed and muttered a little shyly, and unsurely, pulling clothes back into position, and brushing off petals and greenery.

"You won't say anything, will you?" Sean said.

Maggie was taken aback. That this was the first thing he said.

"To Stacey, I mean."

"No, Sean. I won't say anything."

"Thank you." He looked relieved. "I do really like you and everything, but this... this shouldn't have happened. I've just asked her to marry me. And she said yes."

He paused.

"Are you waiting for congratulations?" Maggie said scathingly.

"What? Oh, no! No! Sorry. It's just... this shouldn't have happened. And at your dad's... I'm sorry."

"You and me both."

"You started it, Maggie."

"Fucking hell, Sean. This isn't the school playground. But no, don't worry, I won't say a word. Your secret's safe with me."

They walked in silence back to the house, Maggie

slipping in through the front door while Sean went straight to the garden gate. She marched straight up to her bedroom, shutting the door behind her, and throwing herself on her bed, allowing the tears to come. It took her back to her teenage years, following an argument with Julia, or Lucy, or Jeff. The self-pity she could feel back then! But she had been only a kid. She was trying it all out. Now, she was all grown up, and everything felt very much, horribly, real.

# Maggie

The shock of having seen Stacey and Sean means that I finish my first drink a little too fast, but luckily nobody seems to notice. Paul has always enjoyed a pint, and he's ready to order a second. When the waiter comes across, Paul looks at me, and nods towards my empty glass. "Same again?"

"Yes please."

My heart rate seems to have slowed a little, now that the danger has passed. And they are just here for the weekend, Stacey said. Also, judging by their choice of restaurant tonight, we're unlikely to be frequenting the same establishments.

My mouth is dry, though, and my appetite all but gone, but I've told Julia I'm famished, so I'm just going to have to play along. "A Fiorentina, please," I say to the waitress with a smile, handing my menu over.

"Is that the one with egg?" Paul turns up his nose. "I never did get that."

"Honestly, it's really nice, you should try it."

"Yeah, sure, when Hell freezes over."

I love my relationship with my brother-in-law. He is as I imagine an actual brother may be. I feel guilty again on Stevie's behalf that she won't have a sibling relationship. But plenty of people don't, and they turn out just fine. And plenty of other people don't get on with their siblings, which I imagine could be worse than not having any.

By the time the pizzas turn up (the place is rammed, and there is some issue with staff shortages), I have finished my third gin, and Mum and I are choosing a bottle of wine.

"Julia? Are you having a glass?" Julia doesn't often drink, but occasionally enjoys a glass of wine with dinner.

"Erm… no, I'm fine, thanks. I need a clear head tomorrow. There's a rehearsal in the afternoon and I could do with being back for it."

Mum also won't drink much. And Paul is sticking with beer. All the more for me, then. But I don't want to get drunk, with Stevie around. It's not something I've ever done, and I don't intend to start now. Nevertheless, by the time we leave the restaurant, I bet I've had near enough two thirds of the bottle, on top of three gin & tonics. Way more than I've had before. And that might explain my actions when, on seeing Stacey and Sean again, heading our way, I grab Julia's hand and quickly say to Mum, "I've just got to show Julia something, can we meet you back at yours?" then kiss Stevie, telling her I'll be back shortly, and drag my sister off along the pier by the lifeboat station. If Stacey and her brood happen to come up this way, I'll be trapped, unless I jump for it, but I'm banking on them heading straight past, and I'm relieved when they do.

"What's going on, Maggie?" I realise Julia has asked me this, or a variation of this, more than once, but I've been too intent on keeping a low profile.

"Oh, nothing," I try to say airily, and take what I hope

is a nonchalant step back towards the town, but I catch my foot on a cobble, and somehow end up falling, banging my knee.

"Maggie! Are you OK?"

"Yes, I'm…" But I'm not. I'm really not. My knee is throbbing, for one thing, and it's like the sharp pain of the impact of my fall has pierced something within me. Something that, really, has been waiting to escape all these years, like helium from a balloon. And it's coming, streaming out now, and there's nothing I can do to stop it. "I'm not. I'm not OK," I say, melodramatically, throwing my arms around my worried twin. "I'm really not. Well, I am. But I'm not."

"Maggie." Julia takes me by the shoulders and makes me look at her. My big sister by nine minutes and seventeen seconds, but who has always been head and shoulders above me. "Tell me what is going on. You've been weird all evening."

"Have I?" I really thought I'd pulled off behaving completely normally. "Oh god, have I been a twat?"

"No, not a twat. But I know you. And I know when you're being weird. Now tell me what is going on."

She links her arm through mine, and helps me hobble to a bench, where we sit close together, and I hope nobody I know passes by. And I really hope Stacey and Sean don't turn up again.

# 2009

She was dreading that first Christmas after Jeff's death. Dreading going home, but to stay in Bristol was unthinkable. Lucy needed her, for one thing. And Maggie knew that, even though her mum would put no pressure on her to come back to Cornwall, if she had stayed in her flat, maybe going out for Christmas Eve drinks with her friends and joining some of them for Christmas dinner, she would regret it. She could imagine the ache, returning to her empty flat, and knowing that three hours down the road, Lucy would be on her own in their family home. No, it wasn't even worth contemplating. She booked a week off work, and travelled down the motorway on 23rd December, so that she could be there for her mum on Christmas Eve, and Christmas Day, and Boxing Day – and stay for New Year's as well if that seemed the right thing to do. She had no wish to celebrate this year anyway – neither the year that had passed, nor the one that was to come. What would she be celebrating, really?

As it turned out, it wasn't as bad as she had been expecting. When she'd arrived at her family home, Lucy opened the front door, greeting her daughter with a wide smile. Maggie's keen eyes took in the details: Lucy was thinner than she had been, but not to the point of looking ill, and she looked tired, but she looked so pleased to see Maggie, and the two of them hugged, as Lucy pulled her daughter into the house and shut the front door with her foot. It was hard to let go, for both of them, and both were trying to hide their tears from each other, but in the end gave in, and wept in each other's arms. It felt good. It felt right.

Maggie had never mentioned Jeff's infidelity; not to anyone. She thought it was probably true, as much as she hated to admit it. Looking back now at her childhood, she could see things that she would never have noticed back then. Jeff did become more absent than he had been, for a while. She had assumed at the time that it was his new role, after Rob had left, and maybe Lucy had told the girls that's what was going on. Maybe Lucy thought that was what was going on. Maggie remembered how Jeff and Lucy seemed to have drifted apart, and that anniversary when she and Julia had planned the meal and how it had seemed like a bit of a turning point. Was that all tied up with whatever happened with Jeff and Sarah?

She could go mad, trying to work it out, and back in Bristol she had been seeing a counsellor, trying to unpick it all, and separate her grief from her anger, and her sense of betrayal. She had realised that she felt angry at Lucy, which was entirely unreasonable, and she knew it was no failing of her mum's.

So now, here she was, back home in a house that was missing such an important component. Even when Julia came round later, without Paul, it felt empty. Maybe even more so, because Jeff's absence was so apparent. The three of them ate dinner together, and talked about Maggie's job, and how busy life was in Bristol; and Lucy's job, and how she'd taken up sea swimming at weekends; and Julia's job, and how she was planning on opening her own dance school. Although Jeff had left everything to Lucy, there was some money that she had passed on to their daughters. Maggie had put most of it away, to help save a deposit for a flat of her own, and bought herself a second-hand, but reasonably new, car. Julia was intending to put her money into a business of her own.

"I don't want children just yet," she stated, on her fourth glass of wine.

"Well, you're only young," Lucy said. "Plenty of time for that. And now's the time to go for it, branch out on your own. Is Paul still keen for you to do it?"

"He'd support me in anything I want to do," Julia slurred slightly. Maggie hadn't seen her sister this drunk for a while. Maybe Julia was trying to blot out the pain. Maggie had gone the other way. She hadn't drunk at all since Jeff's funeral, fearing it might make her lose the careful control she had constructed. Although she had a glass of wine in front of her now, the thought of it made her feel a bit queasy.

Lucy was also nursing her first glass. She glanced at Maggie, and they shared a look. It made Maggie feel grown-up. She liked it.

Paul picked Julia up, and came in to say hello.

"How are you, Maggie?" he asked, hugging her.

"Oh, you know, OK. I suppose. All things considered. How has Julia been?" she asked, sotto voce, while her sister ambled off to find her coat.

"Not great. She's missing Jeff, and I think she's really missing you."

"I do miss her, too. Maybe you two can come up for a weekend in the new year?"

"That sounds like an excellent idea. I'll make myself scarce for a bit, and you can have some time together."

"Talking about me?" Julia appeared in the doorway.

"We were just saying you two should come up for a weekend," Maggie said.

"I'd like that," Julia said, struggling to get her arms into her coat. "Oh!" she flapped them around in frustration, then collapsed into a sobbing heap. "Stupid fucking coat."

"Come on," Maggie said, moving to gently help her sister up, and hug her. "Come on. It's OK."

"It's not though, is it? Because he's gone. And he's not coming back."

"I know." Maggie wondered why she too wasn't in tears, but it seemed to be to do with feeling responsible, and adult, and like she needed to prop her sister up. Perhaps the tears would come later. "I know," she said again, and she let Julia sob into her shoulder, while Paul considerately went to use the bathroom.

"We'll get through it, Julia," Maggie said. "We will."

"But he's gone. And you… you've gone. Up to Bristol. And Mum's here, but I'm not enough. I can't do it all."

"You don't have to," said Maggie. "I'm sorry. I didn't know you felt like that."

"Oh, I don't, not really. But I know I'm not enough for her. And I've got Paul to think about. And I really do want to get this business going. I have to leave my job. I can't stand working for Yvette any longer." She had stopped crying now, and seemed remarkably more sober.

"I'm so sorry. I honestly didn't know. I thought you were happy. Well, apart from Dad, of course."

"I am, really. Well, you know, as much as I can be. I'm sorry, I think it's the wine. And don't worry, I'm not turning into an alcoholic." She wiped her nose on her sleeve, stepping back a little so Maggie could see she was sincere. "I've just been dreading Christmas."

"Me too. Me too. Honestly. I'd rather forget the whole fucking thing."

"Really?" Julia looked relieved. "I just always think you're so together. You always have been. Even at school. Me and Stacey, were so into our clothes, and makeup, and boys, and stupid stuff. You always had your head screwed on right."

"I don't know about that." It was interesting to hear Julia's take on things, even if it was ten years too late.

"It's true. You're amazing. Dad always rated you so highly."

"He did you as well."

"Well, yes, but differently. You're like him, aren't you? And I'm... well, I don't know. This is why I want to do it, go it alone. Start a dance school of my own. But..." she lowered her voice – "don't tell Mum, but Paul really wants us to have a family."

"Really? I thought you said he was OK with you doing the dance school thing."

"Well, he wouldn't say no. I mean, of course he can't, but he wouldn't object. He will support me in anything, I know, but I also know he wants kids, and the sooner the better as far as he's concerned."

"Do you not want them?"

"I do... I think I do... Oh, my head's starting to hurt. I'm an idiot, drinking all that wine. I feel sick. I—"

Julia promptly threw up, all down Maggie's front, and onto her own shoes.

"Oh my, oh, I'm sorry, Maggie."

"Don't worry," Maggie said, looking down at herself in dismay, but keen to make Julia feel alright. "Don't worry."

Lucy appeared in the doorway. "Is everything alright... oh..."

"I'm sorry, Mum!" Julia exclaimed. Paul also appeared in the doorway.

"Don't worry," Lucy said, taking control, and it felt to Maggie like she and Julia were kids again. She remembered a terrible sickness bug they'd had at the same time, when they were twelve, and Lucy being on hand with buckets, wipes, glasses of water, clean clothes, clean bedding, the works... Was Jeff with Sarah when that was going on? The thought briefly crossed Maggie's mind before she banished it.

"Paul, take Julia into the downstairs toilet, and get her out of those clothes, and I'll bring some of mine. Maggie, go and strip off by the washing machine, and I'll get you a towel, and then you can have a shower. You'd have been getting ready for bed soon anyway!"

"Sure," said Maggie. "Are you OK, Julia?" she asked as Paul led her sister gently off.

"Just horribly embarrassed," Julia said ruefully.

"Well don't be. It's just us. Me, Mum and Paul. You don't need to worry about anything."

Paul smiled at her, and Maggie tentatively made her way towards the utility room. She peeled the clothes off herself, trying not to look (or smell) in too much detail. It wasn't too bad. Julia had not eaten a lot, and had at least been drinking white wine. Lucy grinned at her when she came through, offering a large, soft blue towel. Maggie wrapped it gratefully around herself.

"Poor Julia," she said.

"I know," said Lucy. "Not good. But not that outrageous, either. And don't worry, I don't think she has a drink problem. Just trying to get through Christmas, like we all are."

"It's horrible, isn't it?"

"Yes. It is. Just unreal, really. But go on, go and have a shower, get your pyjamas on, or you'll be shivering."

It was nice, somehow, being told what to do by Lucy. Reverting to a child for a while.

"We're just going to stay here tonight," Paul told her when she walked into the hallway. "I'll run Julia a bath, if you have a shower in your Mum and Dad's... your Mum's..." He looked doubtful.

"It's hard, isn't it? Let's just say Mum and Dad's bathroom, shall we? It's still theirs, even if he's not here."

"Yeah, OK. Yeah."

Maggie pulled the towel tightly around herself and went upstairs, entering her parents' darkened bedroom. It was strange being in there, and as she switched the light on she saw that her mum had put a photo of Jeff on his bedside table. Maggie didn't know how it made her feel. Sad, obviously. Pleased, that her mum had loved her dad so much. Angry, that Jeff had betrayed Lucy. And then almost surprised, as the realisation hit her once again that it was really true. He really was gone.

As the hot water soothed her, and she soaped herself liberally with her mum's nice shower gel, inhaling the gentle aromas of geranium and bergamot, Maggie replayed the conversation she'd had with Julia. How strange it was, to find out how you really seemed through somebody else's eyes. And she realised how insecure everyone was when they were growing up – even Stacey must have been, but Maggie had been too young and naïve to realise it back then.

It was so interesting that Julia wasn't ready to have kids. Maggie couldn't imagine thinking about that kind of thing for some time yet. But then, she wasn't in a relationship, was she... her train of thought turned back on itself.

The water continued pouring down on her, and the steam continued to rise, but it felt like Maggie had stopped, stepped outside of herself, as her memory traipsed back and forth over the last few months. Had she...? No. She hadn't.

She hadn't had a period since the summer.

Not since before Jeff died.

And not since she had slept with Sean.

# Maggie

"It's…" Where do I begin? How do I begin? I've heard the very beginning is a very good place to start. But there's something in this story that isn't mine to tell. So Julia gets a half-truth, and not one that paints me in a very good light.

"I did wonder if something happened with you two," she said.

"You… how?"

"I saw you, from my window. I was just looking out at everyone, and I saw you and Sean leave together. I kept watch, but you were gone ages, and I gave up looking, and went to bed. You were strange the next day, though, and I knew it wasn't just Dad."

"I was strange? In what way?"

"I don't know. I just think you were very quiet. And distracted. Like something was playing on your mind. It could have just been grief, of course, but it felt different to me."

"And here I was thinking I'd kept it so well under wraps."

"You had, really. I don't suppose anyone else would have noticed there was anything wrong. I wanted to ask you about it, but you went back to Bristol, and became a bit obsessed with work. I never quite forgot, but over time I suppose it seemed less important."

The effects of the alcohol are wearing off now, and my head is beginning to ache. But maybe, just maybe, there is a little easing of the tension in my neck. "Trust you to know there was something else going on."

"Ah, yes, well like I said, I had seen you leave with him, too–" I can almost hear the cogs whirring– "He's Stevie's dad?" The realisation of this seems to hit her like a slap across the face. I nod, silently. "Oh my god, Maggie. Shit."

"I know." I sit glumly staring at my hands in my lap. I feel like the biggest fraud, and I brace myself for her anger.

"What a total bastard."

"What?" I look up.

"What an utter bastard. Taking advantage of you like that. After our dad's funeral. While he was with Stacey."

"They'd just got engaged," I laugh mirthlessly.

"I'm going to kill him!" Julia stands, her fists balled.

"No. Sit down, Julia. It's my fault. I – I kissed him."

"So what? So fucking what? Our dad had just died! We'd just buried him, for god's sake. So you kissed that bastard. He didn't have to kiss you back. Or… or…"

"I know," I say. I am comforting her now. I realise she is crying. For my sake. She doesn't hate me, and I wonder now how I could have ever thought she would. How I have spent twelve years hiding this truth, for the fear that my twin, and maybe my mum, would hate me, but never stopping to think that perhaps they'd be on my side.

We hug, my sister and me, and I have never felt closer to her. Did we hug in the womb, I wonder? Mum says we used to when we were babies, sometimes falling asleep like that, and she would pluck us apart, with fears of cot death, but hating herself for separating us. In the dark, warm night, with the sound of the waves lapping at the harbour walls, and the effects of the alcohol splashing around in my mind, I close my eyes and I feel my sister's warmth, and imagine us in our very own private space, closer than I could ever be with anybody else. Contained and secure within our mum. How could I ever have thought they would turn against me? I breathe, deeply, and count to ten. Now I've started, I need to know she really gets it. The full picture.

I pull back a little, though I really don't want to. "So those boys…" I say. And again, I watch a realisation dawn within my twin.

"Oh my god," she says. "They're Stevie's brothers."

"Half-brothers," I confirm.

"Shit." She puts her head in her hands.

"I'm sorry," I say, with my hand on her back. Rubbing her, as if she's the drunk one, and in danger of throwing up.

"Don't be sorry!" she looks up, anger flashing across her face. "Does Sean know… about Stevie?"

"No. And I don't want him to," I say firmly. And in this way, I take the lead. I'm the one who knows motherhood. How fierce it makes you. How protective. "He doesn't need to know. And neither does Stevie."

"But…" she stops in her tracks, as if feeling unqualified to make any further statement. "Does Mum know?" she changes track.

"No. Not yet. But now you do, I think I ought to tell her."

"But then we all have a secret from Stevie," she says.

"Yes," I say sadly. I hadn't really thought of that. In confessing to my sister, I am asking her to keep something huge from her niece. "Maybe I won't tell Mum."

"It's up to you," she says. "But listen, I won't say a word. If you decide to tell Mum, if you decide to tell Stevie, then I'll support you. But you've come this far, without anyone knowing, and you've brought up this amazing little girl."

"Not so little," I say, with a small laugh.

"No, not so little," she agrees. "And really," she speaks as she thinks, as though she's not sure herself what she is going to say, "he's got his family, hasn't he? And you've got yours. Maybe it's best left like that."

"I think so," I say, at once grateful yet feeling like a coward.

"You're so brave," she says, in contrast to how I feel about myself. "So bloody brave. And you've been carrying this around with you all these years. You should have just said. You should have said."

"But Stacey's your friend."

"And you're my sister."

I lean against her, and she puts her arm around me now. We look out at the shining moonlight drizzled across the oily depths of the sea. I am exhausted, but so very, very relieved. The tears come silently, and I feel like I could fall asleep right here.

# 2009

New Year's Eve was terrible. Maggie had decided to head back to Bristol, and while Lucy had been a little disappointed, she had put it down to it being too difficult being at home, with Jeff's absence so very present. If only she knew the whole truth, thought Maggie, but she wasn't ready to expose it yet. She needed time to think.

Her flat was cold when she got in, and the light fading from the day, the sun already long disappeared behind the tall Georgian building that mirrored hers.

She switched on the heating, and the TV. She'd had enough of her own thoughts on the train journey, and was happy to sink into some kids' film on BBC1. As the air inside the flat slowly thawed, and Maggie felt the colour seeping back into her cheeks, she screwed her eyes and her fists up, not for the first time, cursing herself for being so bloody stupid. So bloody, bloody stupid.

OK, she could be a little bit lenient, knowing that she'd been deep in grief at the time, but she also knew there had been an element of one-upmanship – revenge, even – in her having sex with Sean. And also, possibly most toe-curlingly, it had been to bolster her own self-esteem. For as much as she knew that she shouldn't ever judge herself on her attractiveness, it was there nevertheless: an undercurrent of self-doubt, which turned to delight when she knew somebody was attracted to her. She had seen it in his eyes at Julia and Paul's wedding, and she'd liked it. Never quite forgotten it. How pathetic she was.

Just stop it, she told herself now, sternly; a new voice coming into play. *This is not going to get you anywhere. You are, probably, pregnant. The first thing you need to do is confirm that you definitely are.*

At this thought, a tiny glimmer of hope appeared, like a little sliver of sunlight that's managed to push its way through a cloudy sky. Maybe she wasn't pregnant after all. Perhaps it was stress, and grief, that her body was experiencing.

A pregnancy test. That was what she needed. But she'd have to rush, before the chemist's closed, and they wouldn't be open again for another two days.

She left the lights on, and pulled her coat back around her, grabbing her bag and her key. Outside, there was a thin mist lowering itself gently over the city. She exhaled, watching her breath manifest itself in the cold air.

The streets were quiet, but would not be for long, she thought, as she walked across to Whiteladies Road, which was in contrast already busy, with live music blaring out from one of the bars. She headed into the shopping centre, straight to Boots, and picked up a mid-priced pregnancy test. She didn't want to spend too much, but she did want to be able to rely on the result. Did she imagine the knowing smile on the face of the woman who served her? But Maggie probably looked old enough for this to be a planned pregnancy. It wasn't like she was a teenager. Or a uni student. So it was perhaps a smile of hope, warmth and solidarity.

*As if it matters!* Maggie told herself angrily. She paid, slipped the test into her bag, and went into Sainsbury's to buy herself a pizza for tea, and a few of the basics, as she had no bread, milk, or anything. She put a large bar of Dairy Milk in her basket as well. Whatever the outcome, she deserved a treat.

As she walked back, darkness had fully set in, and the mist along with it. There were shouts from a group of lads making their way down Whiteladies Road – nothing nasty, all good-natured. She imagined they might end up at the Victoria Rooms for midnight, as she herself had done more than once. Now, she shuddered at the thought. This would be the first new Year's Eve she had spent alone, and she quite liked the idea of it. None of her friends knew she was back, and would assume she had stayed in Cornwall.

She let herself into her flat and drew the curtains tight, so that no sign of life could be seen, just in case anyone she knew was passing by. Then she took a deep breath, unboxed the test, and read the instructions.

In the small bathroom, she did what she had to do, and then stared at the test stick, as if willing the line to appear (or not) immediately. Sighing, she left the room and went to put the kettle on, forcing herself to wait while it boiled, then to brew a cup of tea, and then, finally, to return to the bathroom. As she stepped into the room, she left the door open, but when she looked at the test stick, and saw with a jolt the line that she had feared, it felt like somebody had slammed the door shut behind her.

# Maggie

We walk up the hill to Mum's place, holding hands and in pretty good spirits considering everything. For my part, I am absolutely blown away by how good it feels to have shared my secret at last – and at how amazing my sister is. Julia, I think, is so glad I've confided in her.

Mum, Paul and Stevie look up as we come in.

"You two look happy!" Mum says. "What have you been up to?" she asks mock-suspiciously.

"Nothing!" Julia and I say together, and grin at each other.

"A likely story. Now, are you coming to join us?"

"Sure."

"Would you like another drink?" she asks.

"I think I've had enough," I say. "I'll make us some cups of tea, shall I?"

"That would be nice. But hang on just a minute. There's something I want to tell you all."

I have a flash of panic. Is she ill? Has she gathered us together to tell us bad news? But she looks too relaxed for that to be the case.

"Now, I've been giving this a lot of thought. You all know, I think, that I am going to leave my job. It's time, more than time," Mum says. "But what I hadn't worked out was what to do next. This time I've had down here,

232

and being able to help Maggie out – and spend time with you, Stevie – well, it's made my mind up, really. I'm going to sell the house and move down here."

"Really?" I say, stunned.

"Yes. If you don't mind, of course, Maggie. If you don't think I'll be treading on your toes."

"No! Not at all. My god, I'd love it. I…" I stop and think of Julia. How this might make her feel. I turn to look at her. She doesn't look all that surprised.

"You knew?" I ask.

"I knew Mum was considering it. And I think it's a great idea. We've got Paul's parents to help us, haven't we? You and Stevie are on your own down here. Well, not on your own, but, you know… If you want a night out, who's going to babysit? No, Stevie, you're not a baby, I know. And Mum will love getting involved in the art scene down here…"

Julia continues, but I have a question. "You've got Paul's parents to help you?" I ask.

"Ah. Yes. I should have known you'd pick up on that. I'm pregnant!" she beams.

"Oh my god! Oh, Julia." Tears spring to my eyes. I hug her, and then Paul, who is beaming from ear to ear. "You are going to be the best parents," I say.

"I hope so," Paul laughs. "We might need some advice from you. I'm scared!"

"It's a long time since Stevie was a baby. I don't know if I'll remember anything. But you ask away!" I laugh.

Stevie is on her feet now. "I'm going to have a cousin! I won't be an only child anymore."

I know Julia will have glanced at me at those words, but I don't look at her. "I'm not sure it's quite the same thing, love," I say to my daughter, "but you are going to be an amazing cousin."

Mum looks happier than I have seen her in years. "Time for a proper celebration," she says. "I've got some champagne."

"But I can't drink," says Julia.

"And I've had more than enough for one night," I say.

"And I'm absolutely shattered," laughs Paul. "But I'll have a glass with you, Lucy, if you like."

"I tell you what, let's save it, shall we? For when the baby's born? Then we can all have a glass. Maybe even a little one for you, Stevie."

"Really?"

"Of course! You'll be twelve then. Nearly a teenager."

Stevie looks delighted.

We try to play a game of cards, but none of us can keep our minds on it. Soon, Stevie is yawning, and heading off to bed, and Mum is not far behind. Paul goes next, and it's just me and Julia.

"You're going to be a mum!" I say.

"You're going to be an auntie!"

"And do you mind… really? About Mum moving down this way?"

"No! It's only an hour or so's drive. And you'll need her, if you're going to carry on seeing Tony. Who is gorgeous, by the way."

"He is, isn't he?" I smile.

"Yes. It's about time you have a life of your own, Maggie, aside from with Stevie. You deserve to be happy."

We lean back against the settee. I consider what it is to be happy. I love being a mum. Love it more than anything in the world. But I know that what Julia says is true; I need more in my life, and it's OK to admit that. Having my own mum here will be wonderful. I know she'll fill her life with friends and classes and painting, and all sorts of new interests – maybe she'll even meet a new man – but imagine being able to just drop by for a cuppa, or have her round for tea. I can't deny a babysitter will come in very useful, too. I know we have Elise, and I love her dearly, but she is not my mum.

# 2010

"Oh my god, Maggie. Oh, Maggie," Lucy said, pulling her daughter towards her.

Maggie had made the journey back down to see her mum, just two weeks into the new year. She couldn't keep this secret any longer, and she couldn't tell Lucy over the phone.

And in the two weeks she'd been back, everything had come to make sense, and suddenly she had felt pregnant, and, having read as much as she possibly could on the subject, she realised she'd felt the baby moving. A tiny, fluttery feeling, like a stream of bubbles right in the middle of her stomach.

It was real, and it had not taken her long to realise it. In fact, she was shocked at how quickly she had made peace with the idea, and how, unexpectedly, pleased she was. This was not her plan. A single mother? Not yet thirty?

And she had not made the progress in her career that she had wanted to, before this happened. She had not expected her dad to die before she had a baby. But she had come to realise, with what had happened to Jeff, that there really is no planning for things in life – or at least no guarantee that your plans will come to fruition. And, having lost one person in her life who she loved, and who loved her, she could not even contemplate not going the course with this new little being, who she felt she might already love, and who she hoped would love her back.

So she had come down to Cornwall late on a Friday night, and almost as soon as she'd stepped through the door, she had told her Mum.

"I'm pregnant," she said, putting her bag on the floor. "I'm sorry, to break it to you just like this, so suddenly, but I just can't wait… I've been bursting to tell you. I need you to know."

And Lucy had pulled her towards her, and there they now were, embracing in the hallway.

Maggie pulled back. "Are you disappointed?"

"No!" Lucy exclaimed, her eyes shining with tears. "No, of course I'm not. Are you?" She looked closely at her daughter.

"No. I'm not. Not disappointed. I was shocked. But I'm pleased, I think. Scared, but pleased."

"And dare I ask… the father…?" Lucy asked tentatively, knowing Maggie had not mentioned a relationship.

"He's not on the scene, I'm afraid, Mum. I wouldn't even know how to find him," she lied, determined it would be the only lie – but aware it was a big one.

"Well, OK. It happens. And you're a sensible girl. Woman. I mean, I wish you had the support, of a partner. If you want one. But you wouldn't be the first woman to go into this alone."

Lucy's best friend in Bristol, Tracey, had been a single mum for some time, before she met her husband, Nick. Their daughter Amber (Nick had gone on to adopt Amber), was Lucy's god-daughter, and was about to finish her medical training, so was a fairly good advocate for being the child of a single parent.

"Thank you, Mum. For being you."

Lucy hugged her. "It's fine. God knows, life's full of surprises. I think we just have to go with them. I wish you lived closer though, Maggie."

"That's the other thing," Maggie said. "I want to move back. I want to come home."

# Maggie

Soon enough, it's time for the new school year, and the new school for Stevie. I'm more nervous than she is.

"Stop fussing, Mum!" she says, when I open her bag for the umpteenth time to check she's got everything on the list. "It's all there, and if I don't hurry, I'll miss the bus. Look, there's Josie and Toby, already."

Sure enough, Stevie's friends are outside our front door.

"Alright then," I say, "off you go!" I give her a hug and an extra-tight squeeze.

"Ow!" she laughs.

"Photo?" I suggest, hopefully. She looks so smart in her new uniform.

"I'm not at primary school," she says. "Anyway, I've really got to go." She opens the front door.

"I love you," I say, standing listlessly in the hallway.

"I love you, too."

And just like that, she is gone. Leaving me in a quiet, calm house, with a whole half-hour before I have to leave for work. *This is it, then*, I think. *The new normal.*

At lunchtime, I call in on Elise.

"Maggie!" she smiles. "How lovely to see you. Come in, come in."

"Thank you, Elise. I haven't got all that long, got to

239

get back to work."

"I completely understand. But let me make you a sandwich while you're here."

To say no would risk offending her. "That would be lovely, thank you. Just some cheese will be great."

"You need more than that! Cheese salad, that'll do. I'll have the same."

It's good that she is busy, while I say what I've come to tell her.

"Mum's moving down," I say.

She looks up from the chopping board, surprised. "Really? Well, that's… good?"

"It is!" I say. "It really is. I may have… may have given you the wrong impression of my mum, actually."

"Do you know, when I saw her, she didn't quite fit the image of her I had in my mind!"

"No, well, I … I don't know why I did it, really. I suppose I've been living with one big lie for a long time, and it's been easier to try and cover it up with smaller ones. Not really thinking it all through."

"Oh? Well, we all have our secrets, Maggie."

This woman is truly amazing. "We do, Elise, but it was pretty unforgiveable to lie to you. I suppose I didn't realise how important you'd become to me and Stevie. And, I'm ashamed to say, I liked the sympathy."

"Oh, Maggie." She doesn't ask me to expand any further.

"I want to explain," I say.

"You don't need to."

"I know, but… I want to."

And so, I tell her about Sean. And Dad's funeral. And how actually lovely my mum is.

"So Sean's Stevie's dad?"

"Yes."

"But he doesn't know?"

"No. Do you think I should tell him?" I've been thinking a lot about this.

"I can't say either way, whether he should be told or not. That is entirely up to you, I think. And I know you'll always put Stevie's needs first. But he doesn't sound like a very reliable person… and, well, you know I brought up my pair without a dad, for the most part. And they're not too bad! What does your mum say about it?"

"I haven't told her," I admit.

"And will you?"

"I don't know. I suppose so. But I'm so ashamed, especially as it was after Dad's funeral."

"Try and look at it from the outside in, if you can. What would you think if somebody else told you this about themselves? You were upset and vulnerable. It doesn't excuse what you did, but it does go some way to explaining it. I'm sure your mum will be more understanding than you think. Maybe when she's living here, you'll find the right time."

"Maybe." I don't know.

"Do Julia and the boys mind that she's coming to live here?"

"Ah… yes. That was the other thing." My cheeks are bright red now. "Julia doesn't actually have any boys. It's Stacey who has the sons. Sean and Stacey."

"Oh!" she laughs.

"I don't know why I said it, Elise. I really don't. I'm so embarrassed."

She walks over to me, this small old woman, and puts her hand on my arm. "Maggie, I am too old to be surprised by anything much anymore. You said what you did, and you must have had your reasons at the time. You've been living in a bit of a muddle for a long time, haven't you?"

"Yes." Tears of self-pity form in my eyes, but I wipe them away. I don't deserve sympathy from anyone, not even myself.

"We all do, at some time or other. And really, no harm's been done."

"But I lied to you," I sniff.

"But not about anything big! Goodness, it's barely worth mentioning! Has it made any difference to our friendship? No. You're a very good friend to me, Maggie, and like I said before, you helped pick me up when I was starting to lag a bit. So let's say no more about it, eh? Come on, the sandwiches are ready, and you're going to have to get back to work soon. So let's sit and eat, and look forward, shall we?"

# 2010

Stevie – Stephanie Jemma Cavendish – was a beautiful baby, and Maggie could not believe her luck. The birth had been miraculously straightforward, particularly in comparison with some of the horror stories people had for some reason decided to tell her once they'd learned she was pregnant.

Maggie sat up in the hospital bed, with the late spring sun streaming through the windows and bathing her sweet, sleeping infant. Lucy and Julia had been with her throughout, and had just gone back home as visiting hours were now over. Maggie could sit back for a while, and let reality wash over her.

She had handed in her notice in Bristol, and Michael said he was very sorry to see her go. "I suppose you'll want to support your mum, though, after your dad…?"

"Actually, Michael, I'm pregnant."

"Oh!" he had looked shocked. "I didn't know you were in a relationship, Maggie. I thought you were one of those career girls."

"I'm not – in a relationship, I mean. And I am not giving up on my career. I am just going to have to take a little break from it."

"Well, I'll be very sorry to see you go." And he had been very sweet; his wife Janet as well, who had bought a beautiful bag for Maggie to use when she went to hospital, and had packed it with baby vests and a little soft yellow blanket ("To thank you for all the presents you've chosen for me over the years!" she had said conspiratorially, making Maggie laugh).

She had a lovely leaving meal at the Olive Shed, with

all her colleagues, and she cried when they gave her a cheque, for two hundred pounds, saying they thought she'd like to choose something for the baby herself, along with a huge card, which they had all signed.

Looking out at the dockside, it hit her that she was leaving this beautiful, lively city, and it made her heart sink just a little. But then, she told herself, who knew what life might bring? She might be back, one day. She might take Michael's job. She smiled to herself.

Another leaving do, this time with her best friends, at the Blue Goose on Gloucester Road. That was even harder. They had laughed and chatted all night, but it was clear none of them wanted the evening to end. Eventually, Maggie agreed to stay at Mali's that night, fearful that if she said no, they might never leave the restaurant.

And then, just a couple of days later, it had been time to go. It was hard to say goodbye to her flat, and she thought she might never forget the sound of her footsteps echoing around the empty space. When she had moved in, she had been sure that her future was so bright, and now... well, she wasn't sure of anything. But it was a relief to have everything done and dusted, and once the paperwork was completed and the keys handed back to the rental agent, Maggie was surprised by a rush of something that felt a little bit like freedom.

With her car piled high with her belongings, she left the city, with the sun setting to the west of her, and the sky already darkening to the east. She arrived at her family home under a clear, starry sky, with her sights set firmly on the future.

Throughout the rest of her pregnancy, Maggie had not worked, and as she was living with Lucy, she had been able to keep her living costs pretty low. But she wanted to hang on to the small amount of money she had, which she still hoped might help her buy a place of her own one day. She just didn't know whether it would be in Cornwall, Bristol, or somewhere entirely different.

In reality, that small amount of money began to get smaller, as Maggie discovered that even small babies needed a lot of things. The money from her colleagues bought a beautiful cot, and Lucy was very resourceful in helping her source a second-hand pram, and then a pushchair, as Stevie grew bigger. But there were car seats, and baby classes, which Lucy said were too expensive, but Maggie was determined not to deprive her daughter.

And alongside all this, Julia had found premises to rent for her dance school, had a sprung floor installed, and started to take on pupils. She was happy but tired, and sometimes a bit stressed, but she spent every Sunday with her mum and her sister, and her beautiful niece, who became a focus for all three of them, and a happy distraction from the gap Jeff had left in their lives.

Sometimes, Maggie worried about the future, and what she could do in terms of work, but she tried to trust in herself, and think of what her dad would have said. She often tried to hear his voice, and imagine his words, in her everyday life, and sometimes, when it was just her and Stevie in the house, she would talk out loud to him – until Stevie grew old enough to ask her who she was talking to.

And the year or so that she had planned to stay with Lucy became three, then four, but then Stevie started school, and Maggie found some work at the same school where Lucy had once been employed, when they'd first moved to Cornwall. It was strange, the way life came round full circle, Maggie thought, and wondered if that was because they lived somewhere small, where there wasn't really the space for things to branch out in many new directions. But the hours suited her, and she had school holidays off, to spend with her daughter. Whenever she thought about moving out, or moving on, that all-too-familiar sensation would manifest in her stomach, and she realised she was scared. So she stayed, and it seemed to suit her, and Lucy, and Stevie, very well.

Somewhere along the way, they had become used to Jeff's absence, and on Sundays Julia and Paul would join them at Lucy's house, or sometimes on the beach, when the weather was good.

Stevie loved school, and made lots of friends. Maggie found herself drawn into the occasional Mums Night Out. But she was well aware that there were not many other single parents around, and she felt this keenly at times. Sometimes people had tried to bring the subject up – no doubt she was gossip fodder for some – and she had come up with the story that the relationship had just not worked out. When Stevie had asked her about her dad, as was almost inevitable, she tried not to lie, but couldn't very well tell her the truth. In the end she settled on: "Well, you know I still lived in Bristol when I found out I was pregnant with you. And sometimes, relationships don't work out, between a man and a woman. Your dad never knew I was pregnant, and when I found out, I knew that you and I would be just fine together. And we are, aren't we?"

"Yes," Stevie had answered, putting her hand in Maggie's. "And Grandma, and Auntie Julia and Uncle Paul."

"Exactly. We're a big family, aren't we?"

"Yes. Do you think I'll have a brother or sister?"

"I don't know!" Maggie had smiled. "Who knows what life might bring? But what I do know is that, whatever happens, you and I are going to have the best time we possibly can. And I will always, always, be here for you, whatever you need. Deal?"

"Deal."

Maggie felt dissatisfied with her own response, but Stevie had accepted it, for now. And Julia and Lucy had apparently assumed that Stevie was the happy result of a one-night stand which, in a way, she was.

Life took on a quiet predictability, and for a while that suited Maggie just fine.

# Maggie

I feel so much lighter these days. I've had far more sympathy and understanding than I deserve, but if I mention anything of the sort to Julia or Elise, they tell me to shut up – Julia in exactly those words, and Elise more gently. But I've got the message, anyway, and I'm taking Elise's advice and looking forward now.

One thing I am very much looking forward to is half-term, when I have the full week off and I am going to have as much fun as possible with my daughter. Her days, and my days, are longer now, and she has homework almost every evening, plus netball club, and the new youth club, which is being hosted in our community space at work. So I really don't see all that much of her. And I am trying to make time for myself, and for Tony, too.

Another thing to look forward to is Mum's move. She's been down every weekend, and we've been out looking at possible places for her to buy. It's so good to have all this time with her again, though I feel bad for Julia, now she's just about to become a mum herself.

"Do you mind?" I ask Mum. "Missing out on Julia's new baby, I mean?" We are down the coast, in the town where Mum stayed in the summer. The house we're looking at is an old, narrow terraced place, with the attic converted into bedrooms, though the current owners are both artists and have been using the top floor space as art studios.

"I don't feel like I will be missing out," she says. "We're only an hour or so away. And now I won't be working, I can go up and visit really easily. Julia and Paul have plenty of space for me to stay over. This way, I get the best of both worlds. I can see Stevie growing up, and hopefully help you out, too."

"But you're not moving here just for me, are you, Mum?" I know how busy Stevie and I are going to be.

"No, not at all. I love it here. I always have. I used to come down with my friends, you know, before I met your dad, and then a couple of times with Jeff, too," she says, smiling at her memories. "My friends and I had an idea of buying a great big house, with space for our art studios, and becoming the new generation of artists, following in the footsteps of Barbara Hepworth!" She laughs.

"So what happened?"

"Well... boyfriends... money... work... marriage... babies... the usual."

"So now you're going to make that dream come true?"

"I suppose I am!" she laughs. "Though it's a bit different now. A place to myself, for one thing. Which suits me better, to be honest. I'm not sure I'm very keen on the idea of house-sharing anymore!"

She knocks on the already open door of the house, and doesn't wait for an answer. I follow her in. The estate agent is inside, waiting for us. She explains a little about the place and then lets us take our time. It's beautiful. The kind of place I dream of having eventually. Set over three floors, with an open fire in the lounge, and a small garden with whitewashed walls, which the estate agent assures us is 'a real suntrap'. There is a little window in the stairwell, and two big bedrooms on the first floor. The top floor is the real clincher. The two smallish bedrooms have views across the rooftops, and away to the sea. There's a bathroom up here, and even a small kitchen area, from a time when these rooms were apparently rented out.

"This is wonderful!" says Mum. "I can use the back one as a studio, and I won't have to go downstairs for anything. I can lose myself in my art! The spare one can be for Stevie, and Julia's little one, when they come to stay."

"With their own kitchen?" I laugh. "That's asking for trouble. But they'll love it."

"I think I've found my place," she says quietly, not wanting the estate agent to hear.

"I think you might have. I love it!"

"And you don't mind that we won't be in the same town?"

"No! Of course not. You're literally minutes away."

"Well, let's not say anything just yet, let's go and have a coffee, shall we?"

"To celebrate!"

"Yes."

We wander down the steep street, towards the harbour. This is such a beautiful little town, I can't wait to get to know it better, and I think that Mum will be really happy here. We take our time, looking in the shop windows, and meandering between happy holiday-makers. It's still busy, though the heat of the summer has died down now.

We walk to a café above the smallest of the beaches,

and are lucky to find a table in the window. Down on the sand, a young mum is picking a baby in a full waterproof suit up – the baby's face is covered with sand. His toddler sister is running around after their dad. Out in the waves, a shiny seal head pokes up, takes in the view, then in moments is gone again.

"I remember skinny-dipping with your dad down here," Mum says with a grin.

"Mum!" I say. There was a time I'd have been mortified by such an admission, but these days we feel on more of an even footing, Mum and me. We are both adults. Both women. And I love her company.

"Sorry!" she says. "He was a lovely man."

"He was." I nearly say it. Nearly ask her, about Sarah and Dad. And what happened back then. How did she take him back? But it's none of my business, is it? That was her relationship, and Dad's. Maybe he broke her heart. Maybe he didn't. But they went on to be happy again, and god knows I understand now that life isn't straightforward, and very little is black and white. Instead, I say, "I miss him."

And memories of Dad seem to carousel through my mind. Swinging me up high in his arms, on a sunny day. Taking care of me once when I was ill and off school. Teaching me to ride a bike. Messing about in the sea. Reading bedtime stories to me. Taking me up to university for the first time. Helping me practise for job interviews. I watch the sea, the waves frothing across the sand, and I want to be in it, letting the water cleanse the unease I've known for so long when I've thought about Dad. What happened with him and Sarah, I will probably never know. I do believe Stacey was telling the truth about it. I remember those days when he and Mum were unhappy and, with an adult's perspective, I can make more sense of it. He was a good man. Kind, and loving, and fun. He loved us all, including Mum.

"I do, too. Every day," she says. "And I hope, Maggie, that you find something like we had. With Tony, or with somebody else. It wasn't perfect, what Jeff and I had, because nothing ever is. But maybe that makes it perfect. Being realistic. Honest. Human."

I take a look at my mum as her face is turned towards the sea now. She has big brown eyes, and long eyelashes. Her skin is soft and smooth, even though she will say she has too many wrinkles. She's young-looking, and kind-looking, and I wonder if she'll meet a new man down here. If she wants one. I would like her not to be alone, I think.

"Cheers, Mum," I say, lifting my coffee cup. "To Dad."

"To Jeff."

# 2019

By the time Stevie was nine, Maggie was starting to feel just a little frustrated. She had stayed in the same job for years now, and knew all the ins and outs of the office; many of the parents, and all of the children. And she loved being Stevie's mum, more than anything. But she was bored. It didn't much help that Julia's dance school was so successful. It was the place that all of the mums at Stevie's school wanted their children (usually daughters but occasionally sons) to go to, and sometimes Maggie thought that she and Stevie were particularly popular because of this association. Meanwhile, Stevie had no intention whatsoever of going to dance lessons – which was fine by Maggie.

She needed something different, though; she knew she needed a change. And she was taking Stevie up to Bristol for regular weekends, visiting Mali and Leon, who had two beautiful children of their own now, and missing the place, and the people, when she wasn't there. But that would be a wrench, she knew, to return to Bristol. For her, and all the more for Stevie, who was so attached to Lucy and to Julia. She may not have a dad, but she had an aunt, and a grandma, and an uncle who doted on her. Besides, Bristol was big and busy, and full of traffic, and other dangers of city life. Maggie knew that life in a small town also had its risks – and was not without its share of drug addiction, crime, and bored teenagers kicking out at society. But life was steady, and felt relatively safe, in comparison.

It was Julia who really rocked the boat one day.

"I want a baby," she said, as she walked beside

Maggie, along the shore of Praa Sands. Stevie and Lucy were swimming, and the twins had taken the chance to have a wander along, barefoot, through the warmth of the shallows. The year was just beginning to warm up, and the touch of the sun on her skin and the presence of her sister made Maggie smile. After a few rocky years, where they had felt like they were going in such opposite directions, Julia was her best friend again, and she was Julia's (well, if you didn't count Paul, but that was different).

"Do you?" Maggie was surprised. "I thought you said it wasn't for you."

"It wasn't. Or, it didn't used to be. But I don't know now. We're well into our thirties, aren't we? And seeing you with Stevie, it's made me think about things. I've been trying to imagine growing old, with just Paul; no children of our own. It makes me feel a bit… wanting." She put her hand to her stomach. "And I know Paul still wants to be a dad. He says all the right things, how it's me he loves and can't be without, but I know he'd love a child. More than one, probably."

"But your business… could you still do it? Life would change a lot, you know." Maggie hoped she didn't sound patronising – but she felt keenly the impact motherhood had made on her own professional life.

"I know. I really do know. Though I suspect I still can't quite imagine the reality. But we're lucky. Paul works for his dad's business. I'm sure Brian would work something out, so Paul could be a hands-on dad, and I could still work, at least part of the time, and Sally could step in to manage… I think. This is how it's taking shape in my head, anyway."

"Have you spoken to Paul about it at all?"

"No!" Julia laughed.

Maggie laughed, too. "You probably should, don't you think?"

"Yes. I guess he's going to have something to say about it. Do you ever wish you had a… Stevie had a dad?"

Maggie knew Julia and Lucy steadfastly avoided this subject at all costs. And she could tell sometimes they were itching to ask her if she was interested in anyone, or interested in being interested in anyone. The truth was, it was close to impossible to meet anybody where they lived. The men she knew were either teachers at the school where she worked, or dads of Stevie's friends, or married to her sister. It wasn't that she was actively against meeting anyone, but everything was so close, and verging on claustrophobic. It felt like any tentative relationship might be doomed from the start, by the fact that everyone would know about, and have an opinion on, it.

Besides, she wasn't really sure how she felt about men. Sean was an absolute case in point. He had asked Stacey to marry him, then gone off and slept with Maggie, the same day her dad had been buried. It still occasionally crossed her mind that she should tell him about Stevie. But really, what would be the point? And then there was Jeff. This one really pained her. It was buried deep, the hurt surrounding whatever had happened between him and Sarah. And it was a subject she had never broached with her mum, or even with Julia. Maybe Lucy knew. Maybe Julia did, too. And, if they did, it went to show that, despite their closeness, there were secrets still: just as she had never told them who Stevie's dad was, neither of them had ever mentioned Jeff's infidelity – but then, nor had she. Maybe she was the only one who knew; the only one hiding the truth. What would her mum and her sister think, if they discovered that?

She always closed off this line of thought, pushing it well away, to the back of her mind; picturing it like an old, cluttered attic, with dusty, dark corners where her most unwanted thoughts could be put away and forgotten about.

Now, with her sister confiding in her, Maggie felt the familiar guilt. But she sharpened her mind, focusing instead on what Julia was saying. She often thought of how she and Julia had kind of switched roles from what was expected of them when they'd been growing up. She had been predicted to do well, in her studies and work, while it was pretty much written in the stars that Julia would marry Paul, and they would go on to have a family. Now, it seemed, the seesaw might be tipping again, as Julia's mind turned towards becoming a mother, and Maggie's was increasingly on what changes she might make, to pick up her career once more. Stevie would always be her priority, but she was not all that far off secondary school now, and it felt like the time was right for Maggie to find something more for herself.

Julia's second revelation was more of a shock, and entirely unwelcome. As they approached the rocks at the end of the sands, and turned back on themselves, Julia said, "I nearly forgot to tell you, Stacey has been in touch. I hadn't heard from her for ages, not since Dad's funeral, but she sent me a message on Facebook. She and Sean got married, and she's a mum now, too. Three sons – can you imagine?! She's just left her job, and wants to be near Sarah. I get the feeling she wants to get away from her in-laws, too! So, they're leaving Yorkshire and moving back down here – won't that be great?"

# Maggie

The following week, we are walking along the harbour with Stevie, towards the estate agents. It feels so good, the three of us back together again. Stevie is as tall as Mum now.

"We're all getting older!" Mum laughs. She is full of laughter these days, and looking forward to her own new adventure. As we approach the window, displaying A4 pictures of local properties, with bulleted lists of selling points, I see two figures just inside, talking to a woman at the desk. Not just two figures, I realise, spying three fidgeting boys on the chairs in the waiting area. My blood runs cold.

"Isn't that…?" Mum asks.

The woman turns, as though she's sensed us looking at her.

"Stacey," I finish for Mum, as she comes outside, smiling.

"Maggie! Lucy!" She air-kisses us. "And this must be Sophie!"

"Stevie," I correct her. "Hi, what are you doing here?" A stupid question. There are not many reasons to be spending a Saturday morning at an estate agents.

"Well, would you believe, Maggie, we're moving down here! We loved it so much, when we were down in the summer. And Sean's had another promotion at work, and we just loved the lifestyle! So we're looking at those new places, at the new development."

"The Saltings," I say flatly. The incredibly expensive new houses on the harbourside. Right next to my office. Of course. Where else?

"That's it! Sean's going to have to be away a lot, with work, so he said I could choose! And I thought those places looked perfect. Some of the places around are a bit, you know, musty and damp, aren't they?"

"I guess," I say, thinking of my little place. I can feel Mum's and Stevie's eyes on me. "Well, how exciting!" I manage a smile.

"It is, isn't it? You'll think I'm stalking you, though!"

I laugh, unconvincingly.

"The boys will be away at school of course, as well."

"Of course."

"So we'll have to buddy up, won't we?"

"Erm..."

"Maggie's very busy," Mum says. "With work, and Stevie, and a new man." She thinks she is doing me a favour, I can tell.

"Oh yes! Your new man! We can have that double-date!" Stacey squeals.

Oh. My. God.

"Julia didn't tell me you were moving," Mum says, quickly changing the subject.

"No, no, she doesn't know yet. I didn't want to tell her, until it was definite."

"That was thoughtful of you," Mum responds drily.

"Yes, well, you know, with the baby on the way, and you leaving her..."

"OK. Thanks, Stacey, well, we'd better get inside," I

say. "We've got an appointment." And I take a deep breath, open the estate agents' door, and walk in as boldly as I dare, followed by my mum and my daughter. I say a polite hello to Sean, and I smile at Stevie, ushering her in front of me, and emboldening myself as I guide her to the desk, and right past her brothers and her dad.

This is the second time in so many years that I've been hit by the news that Stacey and Sean and their boys are moving to the place where I live. The first time, though I didn't want to leave Mum, I had already been thinking about moving on, and doing something new. It helped to make up my mind, and get me moving. But I've done that now. And I feel like I've put down roots here; Stevie, too. Not to mention that Mum is moving nearby. And my job... and Tony... I have a life.

*This is my place*, I think stubbornly. I already belong here. They don't. And of course they'll install themselves in one of the expensive new homes by the harbour. Right next to my office. It really couldn't get much worse. But at least the boys won't be going to Stevie's school. Stacey's already made that clear.

Maybe I should help them look around for something. Suggest a few places a little further along the coast. Or, put them off the idea altogether... tell them terrible tales of high crime rates, and drug problems. Troubled teens. Maybe I could set the members of Caring the Community on them.

But perhaps it's time to accept that there is only so much in my life I can control. My sphere of influence extends as far as me and Stevie – what we do, and what

I tell her. What Stacey and Sean do is up to them. I know my secret is safe with Julia and Elise, so I can rest easy on that score. But I can't help torturing myself with nightmare scenarios. What if Stevie and one of the boys start hanging out with each other? Or, in the worst possible soap-opera-style scenario, going out with each other? And then there's something else, which has always troubled me a little. I know next to nothing of Stevie's paternal side. What if Sean has some health issues that we really need to know about? I feel sick at the thought of it all. And I can't help feeling that maybe this is all some kind of retribution for me. Did I really think that I could get away with what I did, and keep this secret forever?

What a mess, what a mess, this all is. But perhaps it is only as much of a mess as I let it be. I can't keep running and hiding for the rest of my life. What happens next is up to me. At least it won't be boring.

# Acknowledgements

I'm always interested to know who reads this part of the book! I didn't always, but these days I try to, as I know how much work goes into a book and how important each one is to its author.

I will start with my regular thanks to the amazing, wonderful and lovely Catherine Clarke, who has done all of my book covers, and who I am very lucky to count as a great friend as well as colleague. Hi to Guy, Alice and William, too. You are all brilliant.

Next, I must thank the wonderful people who kindly give up their time to 'beta read' for me. On this occasion, I owe a great deal of thanks to the following people (in no particular order): Marilynn Wrigley, Mandy Chowney-Andrews, Alison Lassey, Kate Jenkins, Sheila Setter, Jean Crowe, Amanda Tudor, Ginnie Ebbrell, Tracey Shaw, Rebecca Leech, and Ann Bradford. There is one other beta reader, who I think deserves a special mention, for putting her own writing aside to do this. Nelly Harper, lovely author and friend of mine. THANK YOU so much, each and every one of you. You give me brilliant feedback and huge encouragement and I am so grateful.

Now for my friend and proofreader Hilary Kerr, who is also a great source of encouragement and support. We will meet one day, and yes, hopefully in Cornwall!

My dad, Ted Rogers, normally proofs my books for me as well but on this occasion he is working on his own book and I hope he will just get to read Maggie in his own time, for pleasure, instead of doing me a favour!

I have dedicated this book to my aunt Margaret, my mum's much-loved sister, who has been an absolutely wonderful support through my mum's illness and since her death. My mum had a very special place in her heart for Margaret and her family, and it's been so lovely seeing each of my cousins become parents (although they are inconveniently in Hong Kong and Australia so it's only been pictures so far). Margaret, I hope you know how much we all appreciate you. Love to Dave, Luke, Fran and Elizabeth too.

I found it painful and fun writing about Maggie's secondary school days! Like Maggie, I feel like I would not go back to secondary school if you paid me. It's strange the way those five years of secondary school seem so very long, when you're young. And how many things can happen those formative times that might affect the way you act, or even how you perceive yourself, for a long time after.

But then, some of the funniest memories I have are from those days, and I made some truly unforgettable, unbeatable, lifelong friends in those years. We really had a lot of fun. Perhaps the pain of those awkward years is a necessary evil...

I really hope that you have enjoyed Maggie's story. As you can tell, there is more to come. There are so many people whose stories I would like to write but I think that I have chosen who I will be writing about next!

Coming Soon:

# LOUISA

(Connections Book Three)

Watch out for the next instalment of this brand-new series, in late 2022.

# The full Coming Back to Cornwall series:

**Book One of the Connections series
(Book Three coming soon):**

**What dark secrets could a harmless old lady possibly know?**

Elise Morgan is nearly ninety years old. She loves her family, the sea, and night-time walks. She hates gossip, and bullies, and being called 'sweet', or treated like she's stupid, or boring (and sometimes like she's deaf), just because she has lived a long time.

Elise was sent to an all-girls' school, which was evacuated to Cornwall in the Second World War. She never left the county. She is an orphan, a mother, a grandmother, and a widow. Since her children moved away and her best friend died, life has seemed increasingly empty.

These days, she spends a lot of time sitting at her window, looking out at the world, as if nothing ever happens, and nothing ever has. To passers-by, she might seem just an old lady, but of course there is no such thing.

There was once a time when she lived a lot... and there are things she has never forgotten...

*Elise* **is the first book in the Connections series: a group of stories whose protagonists' lives are inescapably interwoven, in the Cornish town they call home.**

**Writing the Town Read** - Katharine's first novel.

"I seriously couldn't put it down and would recommend it to anyone to doesn't like chick lit, but wants a great story."

**Looking Past** - a story of motherhood, and growing up without a mother.

"Despite the tough topic the book is full of love, friendships and humour. Katharine Smith cleverly balances emotional storylines with strong characters and witty dialogue, making this a surprisingly happy book to read."

**Amongst Friends** - a back-to-front tale of friendship and family, set in Bristol.

"An interesting, well written book, set in Bristol which is lovingly described, and with excellent characterisation. Very enjoyable."

## Coming Back to Cornwall in audio

The whole Coming Back to Cornwall series is being made into audiobooks so you can now listen to the adventures of Alice, Julie and Sam while you drive, cook, clean, go to sleep… whatever, wherever!

Printed in Great Britain
by Amazon